For the
LOVE
of
Dogs

Kim Campbell Thornton

Virginia Parker Guidry

Publications International, Ltd.

CONTRIBUTING WRITERS

Kim Campbell Thornton is former editor of *Dog Fancy* magazine and has numerous books to her credit, including *Why Do Dogs Do That?* and *Dog Treats*. She frequently contributes articles to the *AKC Gazette, Dogs USA,* and *Veterinary Practice Staff*. A member of the Dog Writers Association of America, she serves on its Board of Governors and on the board of the Dog Writers Educational Trust.

Virginia Parker Guidry is a contributing editor for *Dog Fancy* and *Natural Pet* magazines and is the former editor of *Pet Health News* and *Cat Lovers* magazine. She is author of several books on animals, including *Pet Owner's Guide to the Poodle*.

Editorial Assistance: Kelly Boyer Sagert, Sonia Weiss

Copyright © 1997 Publications International, Ltd.
All rights reserved. This book may not be reproduced or quoted in whole or in part by any means whatsoever without written permission from:

Louis Weber, C.E.O.
Publications International, Ltd.
7373 North Cicero Avenue
Lincolnwood, Illinois 60646

Permission is never granted for commercial purposes.

Manufactured in U.S.A.

8 7 6 5 4 3 2 1

ISBN: 0-7853-2441-0

CONTENTS

CONTENTS

INTRODUCTION

O

f all the creatures of the earth, only the dog has been given the title of man's best friend. Many legends tell how that friendship came to pass. In one, it is said that a great earthquake created a wide, deep chasm separating Man and Dog. But when Man called to Dog, the brave animal gathered all his courage and strength and leapt the chasm, barely making it across and hanging onto the edge for dear life. Man pulled Dog to safety, and ever since the two have been the best of friends.

In another tale, God commanded the dog to guide humans through perils, ward off their enemies, carry their burdens, and comfort

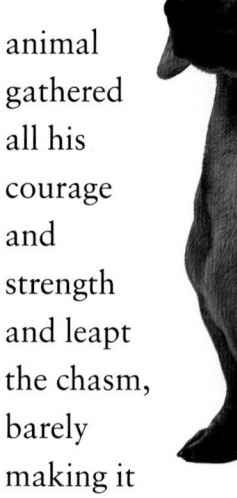

Dachshund

them. So that dogs could accomplish these difficult tasks, God gave them special traits: faithfulness, devotion, understanding, blindness to man's faults, and lack of speech to prevent misunderstandings.

It's not surprising that such tales have developed about the dog–human relationship. Since the beginning of

Rottweiler

the civilized human era, dogs have sought people out, knowing that they could find food and shelter with these beings who were so different from them, yet so similar. As the centuries passed, people learned what a great gift this canine devotion was. Without dogs, early human hunters would have had a much more difficult time finding and bringing down game. Flocks would have wandered off or been attacked and decimated by predators. Dogs helped keep people warm at night and warned them of approaching dangers.

And dogs are just plain fun. Who can resist the antics of a puppy, his

Siberian Husky

soft tongue caressing a laughing face, his squeals and sharp, tiny growls as he attacks a toy? Certainly not the children of long ago. Like kids today, they were probably enchanted by the soft, fuzzy warmth of a found pup. The cries of "Please, can we keep him?" echo through the millennia.

As their value to people grew, the genetic diversity of dogs became evident. From a single type, they evolved into giant mastiffs, furry sled dogs, sleek sighthounds, keen-nosed scenthounds, tiny lap dogs. They developed smooth coats, long coats, curly coats, wiry coats, waterproof coats. In color, they resembled the palette of the earth, with fur as red as clay, brown as earth, black as night, white as snow, yellow as corn, silver as the moon, striped like the grasslands. Whatever their size, shape, appearance, or function, each dog held a special place in

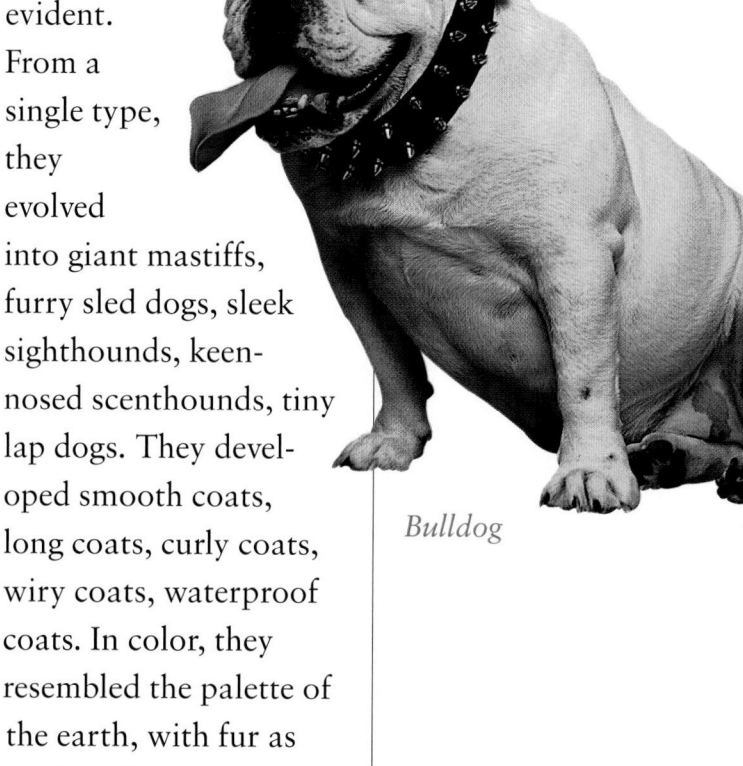

Bulldog

Old English Sheepdog

human hearts and in human society.

But no matter how dogs differ in appearance or purpose, their behavior is what bonds them as a species. Although individual dogs have unique personalities, all dogs communicate in similar ways, with wagging tails and doggie grins, barks and play bows. From the Great Dane to the tiny Yorkie, each dog is genetically programmed to relate to other dogs and people in this easy-to-learn body language.

This consistency of behavior—along with their more highly developed senses—is what has made dogs so valuable to people and so easy to teach to perform a variety of seemingly amazing tasks. Drug dogs sniff out illicit substances, even though the odor may be masked by such strong scents as coffee beans. Bloodhounds follow trails for hours, or even days, searching the ground and air for an elusive scent. Guide

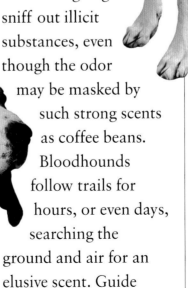

Great Dane

Basset Hound

Whippet

dogs not only learn where to take their owners, but also when they should disobey a command in order to protect their charges.

Assistance dogs turn on lights, pick up change, open doors, and bring items as needed. These are just a few of the ways in which dogs' innate behaviors have been harnessed to help people.

Of course, all work and no play isn't any more fun for a dog than it is for us. Dogs love to play, and they are capable of great creativity and complexity in their games. Dog sports such as agility and flyball are spreading across the country—to the great delight of players and spectators alike.

Golden Retriever

From simple games of fetch to intense Frisbee flying disk competitions, from obedience trials to water play, dogs are always ready, willing, and able to spend some active—and sometimes not so active—leisure time with their human friends.

Dogs have found their way into every aspect of human life. We see them in television shows, movies, and commercials. We read about them in popular and classic literature, and through the ages we have portrayed them in paintings and sculpture, from cave drawings to modern art. Lassie, Toto, Spuds Mackenzie, Beethoven—all are cultural icons, and new ones are created each year.

It's no wonder dogs are such special companions, extraordinarily deserving of our love, attention, and care, which we give readily in exchange for the love of dogs.

Great Pyrenees

Boston Terrier

Chapter 1

History of the Dog

*The truth remains that it was not man
who discovered the dog. Rather, it was the dog
who discovered man.*

—*Stephen Baker*

ORIGINS: FROM THE DAWN OF TIME

In many of the world's creation myths, Dog served as a helper and teacher to people, bringing food, fire, weapons, and speech. How did dogs and people come to be such good friends? The answer lies many millennia in the past.

Previous page: A drawing from the wall of an Egyptian tomb.

Science tells us that the ancestor of the first wild dogs, *Hesperocyon,* or dawn dog, appeared in North America as long as 54 million years ago. Another early dog ancestor was *Cynodictis,* found in Europe. These ancient canids were descended from *Miacis,* an early tree-dwelling mammal that is the ancestor of all carnivores.

In all its wondrous varieties, the dog we know today, *Canis familiaris,* is believed by most experts to be descended from the wolf. This was not the big timber wolf we think of today but a smaller variety called the Asiatic wolf, which was probably about the size of a coyote. Jackals were once thought to be

Salukis (opposite page) are believed to be one of the oldest known dog breeds, and they have been highly prized over the centuries, even in cultures where dogs are not much appreciated. Although Moslems considered dogs unclean, they declared the Saluki sacred and gave the breed special treatment. It's obvious from the Saluki's aerodynamic shape and smooth coat, adorned with feathering on the ears, legs, and tail, that it is a desert-bred dog, built for speed over rough terrain.

In ancient cultures from Africa to China to Mexico, warm-bodied hairless dogs were prized not only for their unusual appearance but also for their medicinal value. The warmth they gave off was believed to be soothing, especially to people with stomach ailments. Unlike coated dogs, hairless dogs have sweat glands and perspire rather than pant to release body heat. This dog (right) is a Xoloitzcuintli (SHOW-low-eetz-KWEENT-lee), a breed that was developed in Mexico.

For family values, you can't beat the African wild dog (below), considered to be the most social of all the canines. These wild dogs, who are seriously endangered, live in extended families in which all members care for pups, and each pack member is treated equally at mealtime. In their complex, advanced social order, a special greeting ritual marks all comings and goings, and males assist in caring for offspring.

the ancestors of modern dogs, but this theory has been debunked.

With their long legs and slender, supple bodies, it's obvious that the first wild dogs were built for speed, rapidly pursuing their prey over open grasslands. But a more striking characteristic was their genetic variability. That may be the secret to the dogs' success as a species: Their adaptability to climate, environment, and food supply, as well as their ability to take advantage of opportunities, brought them worldwide distribution and a symbiotic relationship with people—a relationship from which both have benefitted over the years.

His name is not wild dog anymore, but the first friend, because he will be our friend for always and always and always.

—Rudyard Kipling

The music of the coyote's howl is one of the sounds that defines the Wild West. Even though the West has been tamed, the coyote is still a part of its landscape, adapting right along with its human counterparts as homes and businesses spring up on once-undeveloped land. The coyote is extremely smart and versatile, and this is why it has survived and even thrived while larger predators, such as the wolf and bear, have been driven out of most human-occupied territory.

FROM WILD TO DOMESTIC

*D*ogs were probably domesticated about 8,000 years ago during the Neolithic Period, the time when people first began building permanent settlements and cultivating plants and animals. Although the dog was not the first animal to be domesticated, it was the first to actively seek human companionship. People and dogs have very similar complex social structures, each living in families and working together to defend their territories, hunt and protect their food, and care for their offspring. Perhaps these similarities were what made the human and canine species so comfortable with each other.

The fox is one of the most successful of the canines, with about ten species that are adapted to environments around the world. Of these, the red fox, Vulpes vulpes, is found in more places than any other fox. This sly redhead is small, weighing between ten and 15 pounds at maturity, but whatever it lacks in size it makes up for in brain power. Red foxes hunt in a catlike manner, approaching their prey (small mammals, birds, and insects) quietly on soft paws and using their long, sharp canine teeth to deliver killing bites.

The Dingo has been called a "living fossil." Looking at it, we can get a good idea of what the first dogs must have been like. Native to Australia, the Dingo is what is known as a "feral" or "pariah" dog. This means that it has lost its domestic habits and returned to the wild. When different types of dogs breed among themselves, it takes only a few generations before they revert to type, taking on the medium size, smooth coat, pointed ears, and uplifted tail that characterize the Dingo and other feral dogs.

Of all the domestic dog breeds, the Chihuahua is the smallest. Native to Mexico, perhaps brought there by Spanish traders who had passed through China, Chihuahuas played an important role in religion and mythology. Through their size and diversity of appearance—coming in many colors and having either a smooth or long coat—Chihuahuas display the great variety found in dogs of all breeds.

The first domesticated dogs were probably of one type, looking much like today's Dingo or Carolina dog. The dogs who survived were those with characteristics that were useful or appealing to people, such as speed, good hunting ability, small size, or gentle behavior. In wild dog populations, only puppies display some of these characteristics, but

domestic dogs continue them into adulthood. Such puppyish behavior in adult dogs is called neoteny, and it is one of the ways in which domestic dogs differ from wild dogs. The dog's looks and build were influenced by environment: Cold climates produced heavily coated dogs; hot climates produced smaller dogs with smooth coats.

Ever since people and dogs began their partnership, one of the dog's primary purposes has been to assist in the hunt. Over the centuries, people refined dogs' abilities until they had developed different types of hunting dogs, each bred for a specific purpose, such as scenting, sighting, or retrieving. But for the hunter who could keep only one dog, the German Shorthaired Pointer was developed in the late 19th century.

Nordic, or Spitz, breeds such as the Alaskan Malamute (shown) and the Siberian Husky are similar in appearance to the first domesticated dogs. Their thick double coats were developed in the harsh climate of the far North, and they are built to trot steadily over many miles, having been used to haul the possessions of the Alaskan and Siberian tribes who developed them.

DOGS' PLACE IN SOCIETY

It wasn't long before dogs held an important place in human society. To the Egyptians, dogs symbolized loyalty and protection. In many cultures, they symbolized fertility. And their value to people grew.

As people became more sophisticated and their needs more diversified, they began developing different canine varieties. By the time of the Romans, dogs were classified into six types: house pets, shepherds, hunting dogs, war dogs, scenthounds, and sighthounds. A thousand years later, in 15th-century England, 13 types of dogs were described: greyhounds (which could be owned only by nobles), bastards, mengrells, mastifs, lemors, raches, kenettys, terroures (terriers), butcher's houndes, dunghill dogges (the original junkyard dogs), tryndeltaylles, prycheryd currys, and toy dogs, described as "small ladyes poppees that bere aureaway the flees" (*Boke of*

From cave art to pop art, dogs have always been a favorite subject of artists. The Greyhound—with his graceful, flowing lines and muscled body built for speed—makes for an especially fine subject. This 16th-century sculpture, which originated in Nuremberg, Germany, resides in the Hermitage Museum in St. Petersburg, Russia.

Histories are more full of examples of the fidelity of dogs than of friends.

—Alexander Pope

The Romans recognized six different types of dogs, but purebred dogs as we know them today did not yet exist. During Roman times, dogs were still used primarily as aides to humans, serving in the hunt and in war. Yet even then, toy dogs existed for the pleasure of their owners. And it is from the Romans that we get a warning that is still seen today: Cave canem, or Beware of the Dog. This Roman mosaic shows Greyhound-type dogs coursing a hare.

This tomb painting is from Deir el Bahri, Egypt's Valley of the Kings. While we are most likely to associate cats with ancient Egypt, dogs were highly valued as well. Drawings on tomb walls, which frequently depicted dogs, were meant to enable the departed to continue in the afterlife surrounded by familiar objects.

ack." (In faraway Mexico, warm-bodied hairless dogs served a similar purpose.) There were even kitchen dogs, called turnspits, whose job it was to keep the meat turning over the fire. These different dog types were not like the purebreds we know today. How well they did their job was much more important than what they looked like.

St. Albans, 1486). Ladies' dogs not only served to draw fleas away from their owners, they were also viewed as good medicine. A physician of the time, Johannes Caius, wrote of the "Spanyell Comforter, warm little dogges to asswage the sickness of the stom-

For much of their association with people, dogs were primarily workmates. Only wealthy people could afford to keep dogs who served no purpose other than that of

The ancient land of Mesopotamia may have been the birthplace of civilization, and it was one of the places where dogs and people first began living together as partners. Many pieces of Near Eastern art from Mesopotamia, including the carvings on this Kassita stele, depict dogs and impart information about their history.

In the Middle Ages, only the wealthy were permitted to keep hunting dogs such as hounds. Poor people who owned such dogs were either taxed heavily on ownership or were required to lame the dogs so they couldn't be used to poach game on noble estates. It wasn't until the Industrial Revolution brought about increased employment and income that middle- and lower-income families could afford to keep dogs. Not surprisingly, this is when many of today's popular pet breeds were developed. Many of these new breeds had no specific purpose; they served only as companions.

Dogs have held many different places in human society. At first, they were merely hangers on, taking what they could from the strange two-legged creatures. Then they became partners with people in the quest for survival. As the years passed, dogs grew in value, prized not only for their prowess as hunters but also for their good looks. In the late 18th century, owning a certain type of dog, usually a rare one or one of great beauty, was a sign of wealth or status.

companionship. But after the Industrial Revolution, with the rise of the middle class, more people began to live better lives. They, too, began to keep dogs as pets. By the mid-19th century, the place of the dog in society had reached a new high. Queen Victoria loved dogs of all kinds, and she promoted many new

The status of dogs changed dramatically with the rise of the middle class. In the past, they had belonged to one of two categories: working-class animal or pampered prize of the nobility. Now, led by the example of the queen herself, a third option opened up: middle-class family pet. Queen Victoria loved dogs, and it was through her patronage that many breeds gained popularity in the 19th century. In this painting by George Hayter, the young queen-to-be is standing with her little spaniel, Dash.

Bull Terriers are Johnny-come-latelies in the world of dogs. They were developed in the early 19th century, about 1835, probably by mating a Bulldog to a white English Terrier. The Bull Terrier is noted for his long, egg-shaped head and his friendly personality. For his courage in defense of his owner and his courtly manners in not seeking out fights, he was nicknamed the White Cavalier. The Bull Terrier is also bred in a miniature size and comes in two varieties: white and any color other than white.

breeds. During this time, the concept of the purebred dog with a written pedigree, or family tree, began to take hold. Many new breeds were created, and many old types became standardized. Among the breeds created during the 19th century were some of today's most popular dogs: Labrador and Golden Retrievers, as well as other retriever breeds, the Doberman Pinscher and the German Shepherd Dog, the Bull Terrier, and the Yorkshire Terrier.

Now, as we face the 21st century, dogs hold a higher place in human society than ever before. Most of them are loved for their qualities as companions, but we are also finding new ways in

We derive immeasurable good, uncounted pleasures, enormous security, and many critical lessons about life by owning dogs. It is an ancient, venerable, honorable, and altogether delightful practice.

—Roger Caras

One of the reasons dogs have flourished as a species is their diversity. Dogs can vary so widely in size and appearance that sometimes they may seem to be from different planets. This Rottweiler (left) *and Pomeranian* (right), *an odd couple indeed, show the range in variation among dog breeds. The Rottweiler can stand as tall as 27 inches and weigh more than 100 pounds, while the tiny Pomeranian generally weighs three to seven pounds, although some are larger.*

Here, Gentlemen, a dog teaches us a lesson in humanity.

—Napoleon Bonaparte

which dogs can help us live better lives. Dogs alert deaf people to sounds; guide blind people safely; assist physically disabled people; sniff out drugs, bombs, and arson chemicals; and rescue people trapped by avalanches, earthquakes, and other disasters. However our partnership with dogs came to be, we are fortunate they chose to share their lives with us.

Chapter 2

Breeds

*Depending on his breed, the dog
is considered loyal, brave, resolute,
pugnacious, ever-obedient, dependable,
alert, lovable and fast—to name just
a few of his sterling qualities.*

—Carrie Shook

BREEDS

*I*n the beginning, all dogs were alike. But as they became more specialized, people began classifying them according to their purpose or size. There were hunting dogs of many kinds, herding dogs, flock guards, working types such as sled dogs and watch dogs, and dogs who served purely as companions. Today, most purebred dogs in this country can be categorized as one of seven types: Herding, Hounds, Non-Sporting, Sporting (pointers, retrievers, spaniels, and setters), Terriers, Toy, and Working. There are also many dogs who are mixes of two or more different types of purebred dogs. The following pages contain just a sampling of the myriad breeds.

There are 134 breeds currently recognized by the American Kennel Club; most fit into one of seven categories. The Dalmatian (above left) is a Non-Sporting breed, and the Doberman Pinscher (above right) is classified as a Working dog.

Previous page: *Dogs come in numerous shapes, sizes, and styles.*

*With their unique characteristics and engaging variety of features, dogs of all breeds
are lovable in myriad ways.*

HERDING DOGS

P eople have been using dogs for thousands of years to help control their livestock. Herding behavior—circling the flock, nipping at the animals' heels, and controlling them with a dominating stare—is actually a redirected form of the dog's original prey drive. But instead of going in for the kill, the dogs use these behaviors to control and guide the flock animals.

Many different types of dogs have been used for herding. In the far North, the Samoyed was used to herd reindeer. In mountainous Tibet, small, shaggy dogs, the ancestors of today's Tibetan Terrier and Lhasa Apso, herded animals. Other Herding dogs include old breeds

This Border Collie (above) *demonstrates the instinctual herding behavior found in all herding dogs.*

Opposite page: *Without the help of a dog to watch over and direct the flock, a shepherd's job would be much more difficult, as well as much lonelier.*

such as Collies and Corgis, and newer breeds such as German Shepherd Dogs and Australian Shepherds.

The work they do has made these dogs smart, independent thinkers, but their long association with people means they are loyal and take well to training. It's no wonder that as the need for herding dogs has decreased, most of these breeds have found other jobs to which they are suited. Not surprisingly, family pet is at the top of that list.

Dogs' lives are too short. Their only fault, really.
—Agnes Sligh Turnbull

Border Collie

Originating in the border lands between England and Scotland, the Border Collie may be the most intelligent and hard-working dog around. These medium-size dogs possess a hypnotic stare, which they use to control the sheep in their flock. Shepherds communicate with their Border Collies using whistles and hand signals that allow them to direct the dogs from a distance.

Border Collies are highly active, intelligent dogs. Their desire to herd is so strong that when sheep are unavailable, they will do their best to herd children, other dogs, cats, or anything else. These dogs are happiest in a

This is the original working Collie. Fans of the hard-working Border Collie favor brains over beauty, and variations in size or coat are not important. This medium-size dog weighs 30 to 45 pounds and can be any of a variety of colors: black, blue, chocolate, or red. Some Border Collies have tan points or white markings. Border Collies like to be kept busy, and if there are no sheep to herd, they like to play catch or perform in obedience, agility, or flyball competitions.

Collies come in two coat types—rough and smooth—and four colors—white, sable and white, tri-color, and blue merle (bluish gray with splotches of black). These large dogs stand 22 to 26 inches at the shoulder and weigh 50 to 75 pounds, with males being larger. Most people know the rough-coated Collie, but the smooth Collie is easier to groom. Both have a noble, devoted character.

ented Lassie brought the breed to an even higher level of popularity.

Today's Collies rarely herd sheep, but they are beloved family dogs. They are gentle pets with a sweet expression who like nothing more than to play with children. Because of their size, they are best suited to a suburban home.

home in which their talents are fully utilized.

Collie

The Collie was a Scottish herding dog before Queen Victoria came to admire the breed and brought it to national prominence in England. Later, books, movies, and TV shows featuring the beautiful and tal-

German Shepherd Dog

German Shepherd Dogs have proved their versatility in many fields, including service to police departments and the military, search and rescue units, and as guide dogs. Among this strik-

The German Shepherd Dog is strong, agile, and alert, and her nobility shines out from dark eyes. Her medium-length double coat is a strong, rich black and tan, sable, or solid black. The final touch, naturally erect ears, combines with the German Shepherd's other features to give her what has been described as "the look of eagles."

ing dog's qualities are courage, patience, and loyalty. They are described as bold and punishing fighters if need be, but not pugnacious brawlers. German Shepherd Dogs are devoted to their family, but like any large, strong breed, they require firm, consistent discipline as well as love. Their size and activity level make them best suited to a home where they will get plenty of attention and exercise.

Old English Sheepdog

Little is known about the origins of the Old English Sheepdog. They were probably developed in western England, perhaps from the Bearded Collie or eastern European herding dogs. They

are nicknamed the Bobtail because drovers docked the dogs' tails to avoid paying the dog tax (which exempted working dogs).

Old English Sheepdogs are very protective of their families, but they can be strong-willed, requiring firm yet loving owners. These large

Among the many herding breeds produced in the British Isles, the Old English Sheepdog stands out for his profuse, shaggy coat, sensible intelligence, and characteristic gait, which is described as being like the shuffle of a bear. This large dog may be any shade of gray, grizzle (a darker base coat muted by a mixture of white hairs), blue, or blue merle, with or without white markings.

dogs are good watchdogs and will enjoy a family with a suburban or country home who can give them the grooming and exercise they need.

Shetland Sheepdog

The Shetland Sheepdog was bred down from working Collies to meet the needs of Shetland island farmers off the coast of Scotland. Although they resemble rough Collies, Shelties are a separate breed with their very own distinguishing characteristics.

These small dogs are loyal and affectionate, making good family pets.

They may be reserved toward strangers, but as a rule they should not be shy or snappy. This dog's size would seem to make her suitable for apartment or condominium living, but the Sheltie can be a barker. Unless someone is usually home during the day, multiunit living may not be right for this breed.

The rugged environment of the Shetland Islands produced these diminutive versions of working Collies. Shetland Sheepdogs stand 13 to 16 inches at the shoulder, presenting a symmetrical outline. A long, blunt, wedge-shaped head combines with dark eyes and small, high, three-quarter-erect ears to form an alert, gentle, questioning expression. The Sheltie's long double coat, which has an abundant mane and frill, may be black, blue merle, or sable, marked with varying amounts of white or tan. These bright little dogs are top performers in obedience trials and are responsive to their owners.

HOUNDS

*D*ogs and people were probably hunting rivals before they were friends, but it must have eventually occurred to humans that they could make use of the dogs' speed, teamwork, and greater senses of sight, hearing, and smell. Hounds have hunted with humans for centuries and have developed into two types: sighthounds and scenthounds. Desert-bred sighthounds are sleek and aerodynamic. Movement motivates them, and they were bred to chase and bring down game. Scent-hounds follow a trail, some with noses to the earth; others with noses in the air, scenting the breeze.

The Bloodhound (above) is a prototypical scenthound. This breed has been highly respected for centuries for its hunting abilities.

Whippets (opposite page) represent the sighthound group. Their lean, streamlined bodies are built for speed.

Basseting, a leisurely rabbit hunt on foot in which the rabbit usually has no need to fear, is a sport that is still practiced today by owners of these slow-going hounds with the powerful noses. Despite his short legs, the medium-size Basset Hound is a dog of great endurance, built for following trails over rough terrain. His hard, smooth coat, which may be any hound color, is easy to care for.

Basset Hound

France is home to a number of breeds, including the slow-moving Basset Hound. Their name is their description: The word *basset* means "low thing" or "dwarf." Bassets, who are scenthounds, trailed rabbits and deer and were often hunted in packs. The first Bassets came to the U.S. after the American Revolution, presented by Lafayette as a gift to George Washington.

Basset Hounds are deliberate thinkers, a trait that can be mistaken for stubbornness. Their deep voice can be annoying to neighbors, and they need regular walks so they won't get fat. However, Bassets are mild-mannered dogs who are devoted to their family.

Beagle

This small scenthound is one of the best-loved breeds of all time. The Beagle is famed as a rabbit dog and has courage and stamina in the field.

At home, the Beagle is a gentle and trustworthy friend. Perhaps the country's best-known Beagle is the cartoon

The Beagle is a Foxhound in miniature, with a hard, medium-length coat that may be any true hound color, a long, slightly domed skull, soft brown eyes, long, low-set ears, and a tail that is set moderately high. Beagles come in two sizes: thirteen inch, for Beagles not exceeding 13 inches in height, and fifteen inch, for those over 13 but not exceeding 15 inches. They are cheerful workers and hunt well either in packs or individually.

So popular was the sport of riding to hounds in the 12th century that even monasteries had kennels in which they bred the aristocratic "blooded hounds" that eventually developed into today's Bloodhound. These dogs' noses are so accurate in following a trail that their evidence is accepted by courts of law, and they have been instrumental in bringing about many criminal convictions. Bloodhounds stand 23 to 27 inches tall and weigh 80 to 110 pounds, with males being larger. Their thin, loose skin hangs in deep folds around the head and neck, and their coat may be black and tan, red and tan, or tawny.

character Snoopy, whose love of food and adventure shows him to be typical of the breed. Beagles will follow their nose anywhere, a habit that can get them into trouble if they aren't confined by a yard or leash. Take them for lots of long walks, and they will be your best friend.

Bloodhound

In medieval Europe, this breed was called the St. Hubert Hound and was used to track wolves, wild cats, and deer. Today it is famed as a law-enforcement dog, used to find lost people and escaped criminals.

Their name and fame as man-trailers have given Bloodhounds a fierce reputation, but nothing could be farther from the truth. These mild, affectionate dogs are more likely to lick than bite. However, their large size and baying voice make them best suited to country homes or jobs in which they can use their scenting skills.

Dachshund

Dachshunds were developed in 17th-century Germany, where they were called badger dogs, or *dachs-hunds*. Smooth- and long-coated Dachshunds were developed first, with wirehairs appearing later. Dachshunds come

The Dachshund is the smallest of the hound breeds, yet no one should underestimate her talents. She is keen and courageous, with elegant, streamlined proportions. It is no matter that her long, low body is set on short legs: This dog is tireless, moving with a smooth, fluid gait.

in two sizes—standard and miniature—so there's one to suit any household.

These dogs make good family pets. Their small size makes them suitable for an apartment or condominium, and they are energetic playmates for school-age children. Longhairs are quiet and elegant, wirehairs enjoy clowning around, and smooth-coats fall somewhere in between. Dachshunds are good watchdogs, barking to alert their owners when people come to the door. These long, low-slung dogs are clever, lively, and brave. When

Dark, almond-shaped eyes are set in a head that tapers to the tip of a black nose, and Dachshunds come in many colors: solid red or cream; black, chocolate, gray, or fawn with tan points; and dapple, a pattern in which lighter-colored areas contrast with a darker base color.

they're not guarding the house, they like to cuddle with their owners.

Greyhound

Greyhounds often have been referred to as swift as a ray of light, graceful as a swallow, and wise as Solomon. Their aerodynamic shape gives Greyhounds their speed, and centuries of life with humans have given them a sweet and loving personality. This breed is perhaps the oldest of all the sight-hounds.

The Greyhound bred specifically as a companion is rare, but

The Greyhound is aristocratic, with a long, narrow head, small, fine ears, dark eyes, and a serene nature. Her lines are clean and muscular, even to her tail, which is long, fine, and tapering, with a slight upward curve. The short, smooth coat may be any color or combination of colors; indeed, many people are surprised to learn that these dogs are not always gray.

The Whippet (right) *is a Greyhound in miniature who has a charming, affectionate personality. He is described as a medium-size sighthound whose appearance should denote elegance and speed, power and balance. Whippets stand 18 to 22 inches and weigh about 20 pounds, making them good companions for any size home. Like the Greyhound, the Whippet's coat is short and smooth, and color is immaterial. Gentle in the home, these dogs rev up the intensity when they sight potential prey or play games.*

many racing Greyhounds are finding homes as pets when they can no longer race. The Greyhounds' quiet affection, short coat, and laid-back temperament make them ideal companions, even for apartment or condo dwellers. A soft bed and a long walk each day are all they ask of their owners.

Whippet

A combination of Greyhound speed and terrier tenacity, the Whippet was developed in the early 19th century as a ratter, rabbit courser, and racer and was nicknamed "the poor man's racehorse." At some point, Italian Greyhound blood was added to the original Grey-

hound/terrier mix, giving Whippets their current look.

Whippets fit nicely into any home. Although they are good watchdogs, they are not snappy or loud, and their smooth coat and small size make them an easy keeper. Owners should be sure to keep them on leash during their daily walks, or they may be tempted to chase cats or other small animals. At a top speed of 37 miles per hour, a runaway Whippet would be difficult to catch!

NON-SPORTING BREEDS

*A*ll of the other American Kennel Club categories in this chapter include dogs of similar type or purpose, but some just defied categorization. Thus, a new group was created: the Non-Sporting Group. Although some of the Non-Sporting breeds may once have had a specific purpose, today their most important job is that of companion. This group encompasses a hodgepodge of breeds that vary wildly in size, shape, and coat. They are linked by one common denominator: their popularity as pets.

The Non-Sporting Group includes a diverse assortment of breeds, from the thick-set Bulldog (above) *to the elegant Poodle.*

The Bichon Frise (opposite page) *is a wonderful, loving companion. These playful, sensitive dogs are extremely popular as pets.*

Bichon Frise

The Bichon Frise was well known for centuries throughout the Mediterranean. Sailors took the friendly little dogs with them on voyages, bartering them for goods in distant ports. They were once popular pets of Italian nobility, but by the 19th century they had lost their cachet and were forced into a life of living on the streets, performing with organ grinders or circuses, or leading blind people. It was not until 1956 that Bichons made their way across the ocean to the United States, and they were recognized by the American Kennel Club in 1973.

Her merry temperament, inquisitive expression, white powder puff coat, and plumed tail carried jauntily over her back make the Bichon Frise a charming companion indeed, and her compact size of 9½ to 11½ inches is a bonus. Soft, dark eyes, a black nose, and drop ears covered with long, flowing hair characterize her face. The Bichon's coat texture is notable for having a soft, dense undercoat and a coarser, curlier outercoat.

This breed is habitually cheerful, gentle, and affectionate. Their small size makes them a welcome addition to any household, although they are sometimes difficult to house-train. Their fluffy, curly white coat requires frequent grooming so it won't tangle.

Boston Terrier

The Boston Terrier is one of the few breeds that can be stamped "Made in the USA." They were created in Boston in 1870 when a Bulldog/English Terrier cross named Judge was mated to a white female named Gyp. Their offspring led to what is known as today's Boston Terrier, who is

The Boston Terrier is dressed to the nines, with his brindle, black, or seal (black with a red cast) coat accentuated with white markings. His excellent disposition, clean-cut, short-backed body, square head and jaw, and striking markings combine to produce a charming, dapper American original who moves with style and grace. The Boston comes in three sizes—under 15 pounds, 15 pounds to less than 20 pounds, and 20 to 25 pounds—and his short, smooth, finely textured coat is easy to care for.

nicknamed the American Gentleman because of the similarity of his black-and-white coat to a tuxedo.

Bostons have friendly, lively personalities. This, in addition to their small size, gentle nature (especially with children), and easy-care coat, makes them ideal companions in any home. They are generally easy to housebreak but have been known to be chewers and escape artists from time to time. Bostons alert their owners to sounds, but they are not barkers. These cheerful, lively dogs love to snuggle with their people as often and as much as possible and make first-class companions.

Bulldog

Not just another pretty face, Bulldogs are known for their gentle, loving disposition. This breed, often thought of as the symbol of British bravery and tenacity, was originally used in cruel sports such as bull-baiting and dog-fighting. After these activities were outlawed in 1835, people who loved this breed of dog bred out their ferocious temperament while keeping their resolute and courageous attitude intact.

Today's Bulldogs are dignified and docile,

The Bulldog is strong, courageous, and dignified. A massive, short-faced head, wide shoulders, and a heavy, thick-set, low-slung body are supported by sturdy legs. Her short, smooth coat gathers in heavy wrinkles around the head and face, and two loose, pendulous folds at the throat form a "dewlap."

liking nothing better than to snort happily at their owner's feet while they watch a football game or enjoy a television show. Their short neck and nose make them vulnerable to heatstroke, so they should always be kept as cool as possible during hot weather.

Chow Chow

Chow Chows are of Chinese origin. In early times, they were used as hunting dogs, but—at the same time—they were also considered a delicacy by Chinese diners. The breed made its way to England in the 19th century and was recognized by the American Kennel Club in 1906.

Although they make popular pets because of their teddy-bear appearance and unique blue-black tongue, Chow Chows have an independent, sometimes aggressive nature and tend to be one-person dogs. They are not active, and their medium size makes them suited to most homes.

In his homeland of China, one of the Chow Chow's nicknames is "bear dog"—a fitting appellation for this powerful, sturdy, square-built dog. His compact body is supported by straight, strong legs that produce the breed's characteristic short, stilted gait. The Chow's proud face wears a dignified scowl, and his dark brown, almond-shaped eyes give him an Oriental appearance. This breed has two coat types, rough and smooth, and comes in five colors: red, black, blue, cinnamon, and cream. The Chow is a reserved, intelligent dog who should be neither aggressive nor timid.

The Dalmatian's build makes her well suited for the road work that was her heritage. She stands 19 to 23 inches tall and is strong and muscular with a symmetrical outline. Endurance combines with a gait that is swift and beautiful in motion, producing steady, effortless movement. In appearance, too, the Dalmatian is stylish, wearing round, well-defined black or liver spots on a short, sleek, pure white background. Ideally, this dog has a stable, outgoing personality, tempered with dignity. She is a one-family dog who is courteous to visitors but protective of her home.

Dalmatian

Their spots make the Dalmatian the world's most recognizable breed. Throughout their history, they have been gundogs, shepherds, sentinels, circus performers, and coach dogs, trotting under the axles for miles and protecting passengers from highwaymen, but they are perhaps best known as firehouse dogs, following early horse-drawn fire wagons.

Today's Dalmatians are true to their heritage, enjoying the company of horses and carefully guarding their owner's possessions, including the horseless carriage. They are aloof toward strangers. Dalmatians are best suited to homes where they will receive long daily runs to burn off their energy.

SPORTING BREEDS

O ften called gundogs, these breeds include four types: pointers, retrievers, setters, and spaniels. Pointers were developed from scenthounds, and their job is to find game and direct the hunter to it. Some pointers also trail and retrieve game. Retrievers bring downed game to the hunter.

They come in two types: land retrievers and water retrievers. Setters, like pointers, indicate the presence of game, but instead of pointing, they crouch, or set. Spaniels flush game birds from the brush. Sporting breeds want to please, and they are usually easy to train, making them good family dogs.

Setters are elegant, sensitive dogs who enjoy plenty of exercise, as their heritage required them to spend all day in the field flushing birds. There are three types of Setters: English and Irish (above) and Gordon.

Labrador Retrievers (opposite page) are all-arounders who are ready, willing, and able to go anywhere and do anything.

In addition to their friendly personalities, Cocker Spaniels are well known for their beautiful, medium-length coat of many colors. The buff-colored Cocker is most commonly seen, but these dogs may also be black; black and tan; any solid color other than black (called ASCOB in dog show catalogs); or parti-color, which is defined as two or more definite, well-broken colors, one of which must be white. The Cocker's coat is silky, flat, or slightly wavy.

Cocker Spaniel

For years, Cocker Spaniels were the most popular breed in America. They come from an old family, spaniels having been mentioned in literature as far back as 1368. The Cocker's name is said to have come from the dog's original purpose of flushing woodcock. They are the smallest member of the Sporting Group, standing 15 to 16 inches.

These merry little dogs are energetic, affectionate, and easy to train. However, some Cockers can be snappy if they aren't properly socialized as pups.

Golden Retriever

Like most retriever breeds, Goldens were developed in the mid- to late 19th century. They were created by Lord Tweedmouth—who liked dogs with yellow coloring—using Flat-Coats, Labradors, Tweed Water Spaniels, and other breeds.

This breed is a family favorite. Goldens love children, and their gentle personalities make them ideally suited to family life. They have a strong desire to please and are easily trained. Their coats are easy to groom, but their size makes them best suited to a suburban home with a yard.

Golden Retrievers stand 21½ to 24 inches and weigh 55 to 75 pounds. Their dark brown eyes have a friendly, intelligent expression, and their double coats are dense and water-repellent, which is what makes them such great water dogs. True to its name, a Golden's coat is a rich, lustrous gold of various shades.

From their brown, yellow, or black eyes to their distinctive otter tail, Labradors are a classic among dogs, remaining ever-popular for their good-natured, dependable temperament, versatility, and easy-care coat. They stand 21½ to 24½ inches and weigh 55 to 75 pounds, with males being larger. The Labrador's short, dense coat may be one of three colors: black, chocolate, or yellow. Yellow Labs vary in shade from fox-red to light cream.

Labrador Retriever

This breed originated in Newfoundland, where they were called St. John's dogs. After being imported to England, these dogs were developed to their current form and purpose as water retrievers.

Labradors are currently the most popular breed in America. Their versatility is unmatched: They flush and retrieve birds; work as drug dogs, guide dogs, and service dogs; excel in obedience; and are fine companions. Labs are eager to please and easy to train.

Weimaraner

Nicknamed the Gray Ghost for their distinctive silver-grizzle or mouse-gray coloring, Weimaraners are native to the Weimar area of Germany. The nobles there used them to hunt such quarry as bear, deer, and mountain lions. When big game became less available, the dogs were trained as bird dogs and water retrievers.

Besides being fine hunting dogs, Weimaraners are good family companions. Expect them to be friendly, fearless, alert, and obedient. Their short coat is easy to care for, but they need plenty of exercise.

The Weimaraner is a sporty German import whose medium size and aristocratic features should present a picture of grace, alertness, and balance. He is famed for his speed, stamina, and scenting ability. The Weimaraner stands 23 to 27 inches. This dog's head is moderately long, with long, high-set ears, eyes that may be light amber, gray, or blue-gray, and a gray nose to complement his coat. His docked tail measures about six inches and is carried confidently, as befits a dog from the noble court of Weimar.

TERRIERS

Even an Airedale (above) *has to rest sometimes. The companionship of these faithful terriers is prized by their owners.*

Terriers were bred to go after den-dwelling prey such as rats, moles, weasels, badgers and foxes. Because these animals are tough, smart, and determined, people needed dogs that had double rations of those qualities. What they came up with was the terrier: a dog who never gives up until he accomplishes his mission.

Most terriers have short legs and lean, strong bodies. Their tails are just long enough that they can be grabbed to pull the dog out of a hole. Other terriers work aboveground. They tend to have longer legs and squarer bodies. Whether a terrier's coat is rough or smooth, it protects the dog from brambles and brush. Terriers can be aggressive toward other dogs and small animals, and these bold, fearless dogs give as good as they get.

The Fox Terrier is ever-alert for trouble and ever-ready for fun. These three Wire Fox Terriers (opposite page) *view their surroundings with eyes full of fire and intelligence.*

Airedale Terrier

Called the King of the Terriers, Airedales easily live up to their name. This largest of the terriers was one of the first breeds to be used as police dogs, and they served gallantly in war as dispatch dogs.

The Otter Hound blood in their background, added to give Airedales a keen nose and swimming ability, also gave them a sweet temperament. However, they are terriers and won't back away from a fight. They are good companions as well as being protective watchdogs. They are loving toward their family, dignified and aloof toward everyone else.

This breed is characterized by a certain dignified aloofness toward strangers and other dogs. The Airedale's small, dark eyes are keen and intelligent, and his small, V-shaped, folded ears give him a look of alertness. Covering the body is a hard, dense, wiry coat. The Airedale stands about 23 inches.

American Pit Bull Terrier

Back when dog fighting was considered a sport, people crossed mastiff-type dogs with terriers to produce dogs with strength and tenacity. Because they fought in pits, these dogs became known as "pit bulls." Today, dog fighting is illegal, but American Pit Bull Terriers are still bred for their power, protective attitude, and loving personality.

For the person who can provide the attention, direction, and discipline this dog needs, the Pit Bull can be a fine companion.

American Pit Bull Terriers are courageous, with a playful attitude, and when bred responsibly from parents with fine temperaments, they make wonderful companions for an experienced dog owner. The Pit Bull stands 18 to 22 inches and weighs 50 to 80 pounds, with a short, smooth coat that comes in all colors.

This is a small terrier but a hardy one. Females stand 9½ inches and weigh 13 pounds; males stand ten inches and weigh 14 pounds. A Cairn Terrier has a hard, weather-resistant coat that may be any color except white. Her face is characterized by a black nose, hazel or dark hazel eyes, and small, pointed ears set wide apart on the side of the head. The furnishings around her face give her a foxy expression.

Cairn Terrier

Small working terriers of various types were developed in Scotland for many purposes. One such dog bolted foxes and rats from inside cairns (piles of rocks that marked graves or boundaries). Thus the breed earned its name: the Cairn Terrier.

Perhaps the best-known Cairn Terrier was Toto, Dorothy's sidekick in *The Wizard of Oz,* who exemplified the breed's bravery. Real-life Cairns are good companions, and their small size makes them suited to any home. Like most terriers, they can be diggers, and their independent terrier nature requires firm handling.

Fox Terrier

These dogs rode to the hounds with fox hunters—on horseback. Carried in sacks, they were released when the hounds had driven the fox to earth, and it was their job to rout the fox from his den. There are two coat types, wire and smooth, and the two were considered one breed until 1984.

Digging and barking are favorite terrier activities, and Wire and Smooth Fox Terriers alike live up to their heritage. Their high energy levels make them good playmates for school-age children, and they are good watchdogs. This

Whether wire or smooth, the Fox Terrier is a lively, active dog who is noted for speed and endurance. Fox Terriers stand up to 15½ inches and weigh 16 to 18 pounds, making them a manageable size for a small home. They have dark eyes, small, V-shaped ears that drop forward close to the cheek, and black noses. Smooth Fox Terriers (bottom) have a flat, hard coat that is predominantly white; the wire coat is like coconut matting in texture and is also predominantly white.

The Jack Russell is known for her sense of humor and daring nature. This small, feisty terrier comes in two sizes, 9 to 12 inches and 12 to 15 inches, and weighs 12 to 18 pounds. Her primarily white coat, with markings of tricolor, brown, or black, can be smooth, rough, or broken (very short, wiry fur). If her sense of adventure does not get the better of her, this is a dog who can live as long as 16 years.

smart breed requires firm, consistent training.

Jack Russell Terrier

This game little terrier was created in the mid-19th century by a fox-hunting fanatic, Reverend Jack Russell, who wanted a dog with a lot of white in her coat so she wouldn't be confused with the fox; a dog who would go down a hole after anything; and a dog who would give voice when she had located her quarry. The result is today's Jack Russell Terrier.

These dogs are smart and highly active. Without frequent attention and firm direction from their owner, they can get into serious mischief. Their affinity for horses makes them good country dogs, and their energy level makes them a good choice for an active family who will involve them in their lives.

Scottish Terrier

In the 19th century, several breeds were shown under the name Scottish Terrier, but in 1881, the Scottie we know today was recognized. This Scottie first appeared in America in 1883. President Franklin Delano Roosevelt had a Scottie named Fala, and the breed is a favorite of advertisers.

Scotties are bold and brave, with an inde-

The Scottish Terrier has a deep and abiding belief in his own superiority. He carries his head and tail well up, as befits a terrier of the Highlands, and his expression is sharp, with dark, piercing eyes shining out from under prominent eyebrows. Although most familiar to us in basic black, the Scottie's short, wiry coat may also come in brindle (a mixture of black and another color), wheaten (pale yellow or fawn color), gray, or grizzle.

pendent spirit. They like to have their own way, but they possess a loyal character and make good watchdogs. However, their personality and heritage can make them cat chasers. Firm, consistent discipline will ensure that they are the best of companions, and their size makes them welcome anywhere.

West Highland White Terrier

It is likely that the Westie is from the same stock as the Scottie. Westies were used to destroy vermin, and their white coats made them easy to distinguish from their prey and easily visible on Scottish moors.

The Westie is cute, with a shaggy white coat and large black nose, but underneath that cuddly exterior is a rough-and-tumble terrier who likes to bark, dig, and strut his stuff. An energetic family is just right for this smart, spunky, devoted dog.

This compact dog is all terrier, always ready for a game or a long hike, even over rough terrain. The West Highland White Terrier's white double coat is hard and straight and easy to keep clean with a brief daily brushing. Piercing, inquisitive eyes look out from under heavy eyebrows in a face framed by hair. Small ears, set wide apart, are carried tightly erect. Males stand 11 inches, females ten inches.

TOY BREEDS

This Toy Poodle exhibits the playfulness for which Poodles in general are known.

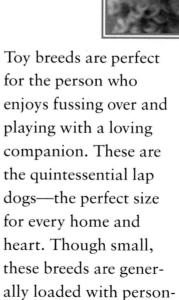

Tiny dogs have been popular in all cultures for centuries for their companionship and portability. Usually bred down from larger types, there are toy breeds of all kinds, from the Pug, a Mastiff in miniature, to the Yorkshire Terrier, whose diminutive body is full of terrier fire.

Toy breeds are perfect for the person who enjoys fussing over and playing with a loving companion. These are the quintessential lap dogs—the perfect size for every home and heart. Though small, these breeds are generally loaded with personality.

The job of early Yorkshire Terriers was to rid farms and shops of vermin. This breed was especially favored by Scottish weavers, who liked the dogs' ratting ability and bold manner. When the weavers migrated south to work in England's industrial cities, they took their little terriers with them. Through breedings with local dogs, they produced a small but feisty terrier with a long, fine, silky coat. Such a beautiful coat could only have been produced by weavers, people said.

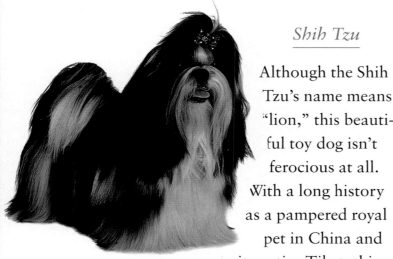

Shih Tzu

Although the Shih Tzu's name means "lion," this beautiful toy dog isn't ferocious at all. With a long history as a pampered royal pet in China and in its native Tibet, this breed has a happy, outgoing, trusting personality. The Shih Tzu's history is found in documents, paintings, and objects d'art that can be traced to the seventh century.

The breed has been nicknamed "the chrysanthemum-faced dog" because of the way in which their flowing coat frames their face. Despite their regal bearing, Shih Tzus have a reputation for being clowns and make fine companions, especially for people in small living quarters.

Toy breeds are known for their charming personalities, and the Shih Tzu is no exception. She has a round head with a warm, sweet expression that is created by large, round eyes; large, heavily coated ears; and an undershot jaw. A heavily plumed tail curves over the back. The Shih Tzu has a luxurious double coat of many colors. In size, she ranges from eight to 11 inches, weighing nine to 16 pounds. This breed's sole reason for being is as a companion, and she fulfills her role well.

Toy Poodle

Smart and proud, Toy Poodles have been known since the 18th century. They are tiny (ten inches or less) versions of Miniature and Standard Poodles, which originated in Germany.

Poodles have ranked high as popular pets for 200 years. That's not surprising, given their winning personalities and the variety of colors and

The Toy Poodle is a true showman who loves to be the center of attention, yet these dogs have a unique dignity and air of distinction. They carry themselves proudly, with head and tail up. Their dark-eyed expression is alert and intelligent, and their dense, naturally curly coats come in numerous colors such as black, blue, gray, silver, brown, cafe-au-lait, apricot, and cream.

Although the Yorkie is a toy breed, she retains a sassy attitude and strong terrier instincts from her ancestors' early days as ratters. Some might say this is a breed that went from rats to riches.

sizes in which they are available. Toy Poodles are perfect pets for an apartment or condo dweller, and their curly coat can be clipped short for easy grooming.

Yorkshire Terrier

Toy versions of the feisty terriers produced in Scotland and northern England, Yorkshire Terriers were developed in the mid-19th century. From their origins as ratters, they became "fancy terriers": show dogs and then popular Victorian pets.

Today, Yorkshire Terriers are smart, independent dogs who like to have their own way. Their brains and determination make them a stubborn but entertaining pet. The Yorkie's coat requires lots of grooming unless it is trimmed short.

In full show coat, a Yorkshire Terrier is a sight to behold. Flowing down each side of the body is a shiny, straight curtain of dark steel-blue and tan hair. The blue covers the body, with rich accents of golden tan on the head, at the roots of the ears, on the muzzle, and on the chest and legs.

WORKING BREEDS

People realized early on that dogs could be invaluable assistants to the human race. So, over the centuries, people created specific breeds to fill a variety of specialized needs, from pulling milk carts to catching criminals. Even today, we are constantly finding new jobs at which dogs excel, such as arson detecting and hearing assistance.

The proud Working breeds have a varied history. Some, like the Great Dane, come from ancient stock, while others, like the Doberman Pinscher, Boxer, and Rottweiler, are creations of the late-19th century. Many of these dogs make fine family companions for those who can give them the structure and guidance they need.

The Great Dane's size deters most people and other dogs from messing with it. This is a gentle breed, but one that is courageous and can more than hold its own (above).

Dobermans (opposite page) *have a dangerous reputation, but they are lovers to those who know them.*

The Akita is a dignified and courageous dog. His massive head forms a blunt triangle, with a deep muzzle, small eyes, and erect ears. Balancing the head is a large, curled tail, which he carries over his back or against his flank. The Akita's double coat covers a muscular body and a wide, deep chest. He may be any color, including white, brindle, or pinto. This is a large breed, with males standing 26 to 28 inches, females 24 to 26 inches.

Akita

In their native land of Japan, Akitas are considered a national monument. Known for centuries as versatile hunting dogs, they were highly prized and were fed and cared for with great ceremony. Even today, Akitas are symbols of good health, happiness, and long life.

These brave, dignified, alert dogs are protective of their home and aggressive toward other dogs and sometimes people. Their size and power necessitate an experienced owner to provide the firm, consistent, yet loving discipline they require.

Boxer

The Boxer is descended from mastiff-type dogs that were known in Europe from the 16th century, but the breed was developed to its modern form in late 19th-century Germany. Their incredible courage made Boxers one of the first breeds trained for police work.

Their heritage makes Boxers alert, fearless watchdogs, and they are calm and patient with children, although they can also be rowdy playmates for school-age kids. They have a short, easy-care coat and—

The self-assured Boxer is always on alert. She is playful with her family but wary toward strangers. This medium-size dog is strong and squarely built, with hard muscles under a tight-fitting coat of fawn or brindle. Her chiseled head has a wrinkled forehead, a broad, blunt muzzle, and dark brown eyes, and her expression is attentive. To give a more vigilant appearance, the Boxer's ears usually are cropped and her tail docked, but more and more people are choosing to keep the ears natural.

with proper training—are generally well-behaved. Their size and high energy level make them best suited to a suburban home where they will get plenty of exercise.

Doberman Pinscher

Named for their creator, tax collector Louis Dobermann, this breed was developed in the late 1860s as personal guardians to protect Dobermann from unhappy taxpayers and encourage reluctant ones to pay up. Breeds Dobermann used to create his superdog included shorthaired shepherd-type dogs, Rottweilers, Black and Tan Terriers, German Pinschers, and Greyhounds.

Doberman Pinschers are prized for their elegance, intelligence, and power. They love being with their owners and are always underfoot. This breed trains easily from an early age and is very sensitive; firm commands work well with Dobermans, but yelling upsets them. Because they are so large and strong, training is important. They are patient with children, and their short, sleek coats are easy to groom. Dobermans are best suited to suburban homes where they will get plenty of exercise.

His smooth, clean lines give the Doberman an air of nobility and the look of a well-trained athlete. This is a muscular dog, built for endurance and speed, who carries himself proudly. His dark, almond-shaped eyes are set in a long, wedge-shaped head, with ears that are usually cropped and carried erect. His docked tail wriggles in excitement when he is with his family. This breed's hard, smooth coat may be black, red, blue, or fawn (otherwise known as Isabella).

The Great Dane's height and weight make her the largest of dog breeds. These giants stand 30 to 32 inches for males, 28 to more than 30 inches for females. Some Great Danes have been known to weigh more than 200 pounds. The Great Dane has a lively, intelligent expression that belies her fearsome appearance. Her long, rectangular head features a black or black-spotted nose, dark eyes, and ears that are either left folded forward close to the cheek or cropped to be high-set.

Great Dane

Rightly described as the Apollo of dogs, the Great Dane is a regal combination of power and dignity. The breed was developed in Germany about 400 years ago and is a descendant of mastiff-type dogs.

Originally put to use as boar hounds, Great Danes today are primarily companion dogs. Despite their great size, they are just as happy in a condominium as on a country estate, as long as they get a daily walk. Their sweeping tail can cause great destruction, however, so breakables should be kept out of reach. As with any dog, boredom can lead to mischief-making, and a dog this size can do a lot of mischief. The short coat is easy to groom, but this dog can eat you out of house and home!

Great Pyrenees

Not all dogs who work with livestock herd them. Many large dogs—among them the beautiful white Great Pyrenees—were developed to guard livestock from predators. Bred in mountain pastures, Great Pyrenees became devoted guardians of their flocks and developed into

It's not surprising that the Great Pyrenees was chosen as the court dog in 17th-century France. These dogs are famed not only for their capability as flock guards but also for their beauty. Except for his color and floppy ears, his appearance is like that of a brown bear, with a somewhat rectangular body and a wedge-shaped head with a slightly rounded crown. His eyes are a rich, dark brown, and his V-shaped ears have rounded tips. His white coat may have badger, gray, or tan markings.

The Rottweiler is admired for her powerful, robust build. This dog is strong and agile, with great endurance. Males stand 24 to 27 inches, females 22 to 25 inches. The Rottweiler's medium-length head is broad between the ears, and dark brown almond-shaped eyes give the breed a noble expression. This is a confident, intelligent dog who knows her strength.

an incomparable help to the shepherds.

These territorial dogs are protective yet gentle. Their heritage makes them independent thinkers, but they are loyal and patient with their family. A dog this size needs firm early training and plenty of exercise. The thick double coat requires regular brushing. The Great Pyrenees is best suited to a suburban or country home.

Rottweiler

This handsome dog with the black and rust coloring is believed to be a descendant of Roman drover dogs who came into Germany with their con-quering masters. The breed as it is known today was developed in Germany in the early 20th century for use as police dogs.

Ideally, Rottweilers are calm, confident dogs, self-assured and aloof toward strangers. They are protective of their home and family, but their large size requires an experienced owner who can give them firm early training. They like to be useful and excel at many activities.

Saint Bernard

Famed as the whisky-bearing rescuer of the Alps, the giant Saint Bernard was used for centuries to guard and herd livestock and pull carts. When Bernard of

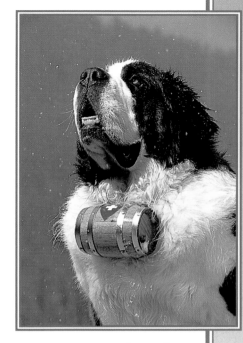

A giant among dogs, the Saint Bernard has an imposing presence. He is tall and muscular, with an intelligent expression. Friendly dark brown eyes gaze out from a wide, massive head. This breed has two coat types: long and short. Whatever its length, the dense coat may be white with red or red with white, and the chest, feet, and tail tip are white. Some Saint Bernards have a dark mask on the head and ears. Males stand 27½ inches, females 25 inches.

It is said that Samoyeds (right) carry the spirit of Christmas in their face and heart the whole year through. Their heavy, weather-resistant double coat is either pure white, white and biscuit, cream, or all biscuit (a cream or light fawn color), and the hair tips have an icy sheen. This dog's face lights up when she sights something of interest; her ears stand erect, her dark eyes sparkle, and her mouth curves up to form the "Samoyed smile." She moves at a trot, with a quick, agile stride. The Samoyed is a smart, gentle, loyal companion who wins the hearts of all.

Menthon (St. Bernard) built a resting place for weary travelers in the treacherous mountains, his monks discovered that the local dogs were of great use in helping find people who were lost or injured. Today, these dogs can still be found at the monastery.

This is a tall, powerful dog with a gentle temperament. This breed can weigh from 110 to 200 pounds or more, so early training is necessary—before they grow too big to control.

Samoyed

A smile is the Samoyed's trademark expression. These beautiful, white, fluffy dogs originated in the far North, where they herded reindeer

and pulled sleds for the nomadic Samoyede and Nentsy tribes of Siberia. When Samoyeds were introduced to England in the early 20th century, they became great favorites of Queen Alexandra.

Samoyeds are smart, gentle dogs who love

The Siberian Husky is described as a medium-size working dog, quick and light on his feet and free and graceful in action. A mischievous but friendly expression shines out from brown or blue eyes, and he carries a well-furred tail over his back. Triangular ears sit high on his head, gracing him with a look of keen interest. The Siberian's medium-length double coat may be any color.

children. They are renowned for their beauty and sweetness, but their coats require frequent brushing and shed heavily in spring and summer. Samoyeds are highly active dogs best suited to a suburban home where they will receive plenty of attention and exercise.

Siberian Husky

The Chukchi people developed small dogs with thick, off-standing coats to pull loads for long distances over the harsh Siberian peninsula. These dogs were the ancestors of today's Siberian Huskies. In 1925, Siberian Huskies made a name for themselves when relay teams of dogs raced a thousand miles to bring much-needed diphtheria serum to Nome, Alaska, to stop an epidemic.

Siberian Huskies are beautiful, friendly, and gentle, but they are also stubborn, independent, and difficult to train. True to their heritage, they like to run and may bolt at any time. Siberians are good with children, but they may be predatory toward small animals such as cats. This high-energy breed requires a firm hand and intense daily exercise.

The one absolutely unselfish friend that man can have in this selfish world, the one that never deserts him, the one that never proves ungrateful or treacherous, is his dog.

—George Graham Vest

MIXED BREEDS

People have been mixing breeds for centuries to create just the right dog for their needs, but today most mixed breeds are the results of accidental breedings. Some people believe that mixed breeds are healthier than purebreds, but many mixed breeds are prone to the same health problems as their blue-blooded counterparts.

Poodle mixes are popular, with such common combinations as cockapoos (Cocker Spaniel/Poodle mixes), pekeapoos (Pekingese/Poodle mixes) and schnoodles (Miniature Schnauzer/Poodle mixes). Commonly found larger mixes include Collie, shepherd, and retriever crosses, but a mix of any breed is possible.

If your desire is for a truly unique yet inexpensive dog, you can't do better than to adopt a mixed breed from your local animal shelter. Whatever you are looking for in a dog, the right one is out there, just waiting to love you.

Mixed breeds can be large or small, longhaired or shorthaired, and come in all colors of the rainbow. They may combine the wiry coat and energetic nature of a terrier with the sweetness and small size of a Miniature Poodle, or they may blend the rough coat of a Collie with the shape of a German Shepherd. Anything's possible!

Chapter 3

Puppy Love

*My little dog—a heartbeat
at my feet.*

—*Edith Wharton*

CHOOSING THE RIGHT PUPPY

Previous page: A group of yellow Labrador Retriever pups.

Buying a puppy is a special adventure. This squirming ball of fluff will grow up to bring you a lifetime of fun and friendship. You can look forward to walks in the park, cuddles on the sofa, and soft puppy kisses in the morning. But before these good times can happen, the right match must be made between puppy and family. Dogs are individuals, and no two are alike. Each pup has special needs regarding companionship, guidance, and activity.

Choosing the right dog is an exercise in patience and good research. By reading about different breeds

Nothing is sweeter than the friendship between a boy and his dog—unless it's the friendship between a girl and her dog! It's obvious that this boy and his Cocker Spaniel puppy have a special relationship. Even very young children can learn to pet puppies gently and not pull their tails or hold them upside down.

As they nurse, puppies bond with their mother. A mother's milk contains an important substance called colostrum, which helps protect the pups from disease until they receive their vaccinations. When the puppies are about four weeks old, the mother starts weaning them from her milk and onto solid food. Pictured are a Labrador Retriever and her pups.

Terriers are full of spunk—especially the Jack Russell. These smart dogs are popular on horse farms and have gained fame from their appearances in movies and television shows. If you choose to share your home with a Jack Russell Terrier, be prepared for him to lead you on a merry chase. These dogs like to be busy, and they will make up their own entertainment if it isn't provided for them. Start teaching them early in puppyhood, or it is they who will hold the leash, not you.

A dog is like an eternal Peter Pan, a child who never grows old and who therefore is always available to love and be loved.
—Aaron Katcher

and asking breeders and other owners lots of well-thought-out questions, you can ensure a match made in heaven. Things to consider are your family's lifestyle (busy or laid-back, children or no children), the amount of grooming you are willing or able to do, and what kind of

interaction with your dog you desire (jogging every day or vegging out in front of the television). For instance, Sporting, Working, Northern, and Herding breeds are generally good choices for very active families who enjoy spending time at such activities as hiking,

Even in repose, this yellow Labrador puppy is keeping an eye on things. Dogs are extremely observant, and one of the ways they learn is by watching everything that goes on around them. They are very good at reading body language and tone of voice. It's no wonder we sometimes think they understand English or can read our minds.

Puppies are like magicians—they pop up where you least expect them. In partnership with a little boy, they can get into all kinds of trouble, but that's part of the fun of canine companionship. Supervise playtime carefully so that everyone has a good time and no one gets hurt. This puppy is a Basenji, an African hound.

long walks, jogging, or running and who wish to include their dogs in their fun times.

Many people assume that a Toy breed is a good choice for a child's pet because of its size, but often these breeds are fragile and can be easily injured if handled improperly. These dogs may be better suited to a home with older children or no children. Terriers, Non-Sporting breeds, and Hounds have varying energy levels. Jack Russell Terri-

A dog is better than I am, for he has love and does not judge.

—Abba Xanthias

ers, Dalmatians, and Whippets have high exercise requirements, while Bulldogs and Basset Hounds are more likely to enjoy a relaxed lifestyle. West Highland White Terriers and Scottish Terriers fall somewhere in between these extremes. A family with small children should look for a patient but fun-loving breed such as a Golden Retriever, but no dog should be expected to put up with children who hit him or pull his hair, ears, or tail. By teaching children how to pet the dog gently and by carefully supervising play between the two, you can watch a wonderful relationship develop.

These puppies are just waiting for good times with their new owners. Puppies are eager to please, and they learn quickly, so don't waste any time in teaching them their role as best friend. Using treats and praise, you can teach your puppy to come running when you call, to sit nicely, and to always look to you for good things. After a playful learning session, you and your pup can stretch out for a nice nap, dreaming of all the fun you have to look forward to. Pictured (from left) are an English Springer Spaniel, a Beagle, and a Golden Retriever.

EXPLORING THE WORLD

Once you have chosen the dog that is just right for your family, the fun really begins. Ideally, your puppy will come to you at eight to ten weeks of age, healthy and ready to learn about her new life. From her mother, brothers, and sisters, your puppy has learned how to interact with other dogs. Now, it's your turn to teach the puppy how to get along with people and how to react to the world around her.

Nothing is more fun than introducing a puppy to new people, places, and things. The expression on her face

All puppies are adorable, but not every breed is the right one for every family. Many people are attracted to Dalmatians because of their striking spots and their appearance in the Disney film 101 Dalmatians, but these large dogs can be a handful. Dalmatian owners must be prepared for their health, exercise, and training needs.

Who knows what lurks under all that snow? Maybe a mouse, maybe even a rabbit! Pouncing is a puppy's way of practicing her hunting skills. For the Samoyed pictured here, being in the snow is a way of life. In her icy Arctic homeland, one of the Samoyed's duties was to herd reindeer. This breed is said to carry in its face and heart the spirit of Christmas the whole year 'round.

No doubt this Siberian Husky puppy feels right at home in the white, fluffy snow. His ancestors came from the cold, harsh land of Siberia, where they were used as long-distance sled dogs. It's not unusual to see a Siberian dig a cozy snow hole, curl up, and use that fluffy tail as a very convenient nose warmer.

as she explores her surroundings and meets the mail carrier, the veterinarian, and the neighbors next door will be priceless. Be sure you have a camera ready to capture the memories! Take your pup for rides in the car, to puppy play parties with other new dog owners, or to a

Few can resist a puppy. Their innocent faces and trusting disposition make us want only to love and protect them. The energy of a young puppy can often seem boundless, although this chocolate-colored Labrador Retriever seems to be taking a brief respite from puppy play.

nearby park or playground. Each new experience will delight her puppy senses. Praise her when she investigates new people and things.

If your puppy has a positive introduction to life in all its infinite variety, she will grow up to be friendly but not easily frightened.

GROWING UP

*P*hysically, your puppy will grow rapidly, but emotionally he will remain a puppy until he is about two years old. As your pup grows and matures, he will go through an awkward teenage stage, then will acquire his adult size, coat, and personality. Each stage is special, and if you know what to expect you will enjoy watching your pup develop into a grown-up dog.

From two to four months of age, puppies learn rapidly, soaking up all kinds of information. This is a good time to enroll in a puppy kindergarten class, where the two of you can play with other puppies and people and learn together about house-training and grooming. Between four and six months of age, your pup's permanent teeth will come in. This

Few things are as entertaining as watching a puppy romp in the snow (above), especially for the first time. Once they become used to this new ground covering, they quickly learn its joys, digging holes, kicking it up, and collecting snowflakes on their whiskers.

Puppies, like this Cairn Terrier (opposite page), love to explore, always running ahead to see what's over the next rise. Doing things together will help the two of you develop that special bond known only to dog and human.

To be liked is very human. One of the reasons why we like dogs is that dogs are so ready to like us. A dog can find, even in the most worthless of us, something to believe in.

—E.V. Lucas

What could be more precious than a Beagle puppy? These small scenthounds are popular pets, loved for their friendly personalities and never-ending energy. Here, this pup sprawls in a soft chair, taking a break from sniffing, roaming, and howling, three of the things Beagles do best.

is a trying time for both of you. Your pup's teeth will hurt, and your wallet may hurt when he chews up expensive shoes and furniture. Be patient, be watchful, and keep plenty of tough chew toys around. This is also the time that your pup will reach sex-

ual maturity. Spaying or neutering your puppy at this age can help reduce problem behavior during the teen months.

When "teenagerhood" kicks in (usually around six months), expect your puppy to start testing his boundaries. The

In addition to choosing the right breed, it's also important to choose the right puppy from a litter. Some puppies are outgoing and confident, some are cautious and careful, some are laid-back and just like to enjoy life. Ask the breeder to help you find the puppy that best suits your personality and lifestyle. Pictured below are Rhodesian Ridgeback puppies, whose ancestors were bred to hunt lions in Africa. Not surprisingly, they'll grow up to be large hounds with good-natured yet fearless personalities.

Even the most rambunctious puppy winds down at some point (above). Help strengthen the bond between you by allowing your pup to sleep in your bedroom. It will help the little rascal feel like part of the family, and you will be instantly available for a morning walk.

important thing to know is that this is normal behavior, and that it won't last forever. Keep a good sense of humor, and channel your pup's energy, assertiveness, and curiosity into activities that test his brain and his body. Treats, praise, and fun games are all positive ways to motivate good behavior. Be patient and consis-

tent, and one day you will find that you are the proud owner of a lovable, well-behaved adult dog.

THE PERFECT PUPPY

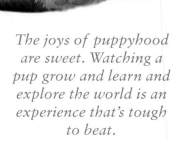

Producing the perfect dog is an ongoing enterprise, but the rewards are well worth it. People and dogs have been friends for thousands of years, and for good reason. A dog is always there; always loving, always understanding. She doesn't care what you look like or how much money you make. A dog cuddles up to you when it's cold and pants with you when it's hot. She's always up for a game of catch, and she won't tell anyone that you watch soap operas and talk shows all day long. So as you enter into this special relationship, be a strong leader and patient teacher to your new best friend. Your puppy will do her part—you can count on it.

The joys of puppyhood are sweet. Watching a pup grow and learn and explore the world is an experience that's tough to beat.

From their mother and littermates, puppies learn how to interact with other dogs. Usually, it's best if they all stay together until about eight weeks of age. That way, the mother has plenty of time to teach her pups everything they need to know to grow up to become successful dogs.

Chapter 4

Dog Behavior

*Man and dog,
an inevitable mix,
is a powerful reason
for celebration.*

—Roger Caras

MAN'S BEST FRIEND

*B*est friend. Just two words, but words rich in meaning, especially when used by a dedicated owner to describe the special relationship between people and dogs. Dogs truly are humans' best friends. They warm our hearts, make us laugh, and comfort us when we are sad. It's as if dogs are endowed with a unique, God-given talent for being a friend. To be sure, friendship isn't something dogs learn or are trained for, like a trick. It flows naturally from their hearts, much to the benefit of all people. The strong bond between a dog and his owner is a natural outgrowth of the way a dog thinks.

Previous page: A Fox Terrier demonstrates his begging technique.

Dogs are loving, affectionate, and friendly to their human counterparts (above).

Some secrets should only be shared with a best friend (opposite page). *Not only are dogs great listeners, they won't tell your problems to anyone else, and they accept you no matter what. The quality of a dog's friendship is unmatched by any other.*

DOGS WILL BE DOGS

The strength of the bond between dogs and people is not surprising when we consider the dog's heritage of togetherness, not only with other dogs but also with people. Even though there are hundreds of breeds of dogs and innumerable mixed breeds, they all have the same basic instincts and behaviors: a strong desire for companionship, the need to protect a territory, and a complex way of communicating, using both body language and sound. So although each breed of dog has a definite personality and each dog is unique, these common

When they aren't busy chasing squirrels or digging holes, dogs like to just kick back and relax, stretching out in a position that shouts of comfort and ease. We could learn a lot from them about stress reduction. This happy dog is obviously enjoying himself enormously, without a care in the world.

These Golden Retrievers obviously love their toys. But what dog doesn't? Play, and the toys that go along with it, is an integral part of the canine personality. While some dogs are more serious than others, most dogs would give their canine teeth for an afternoon of play. Play begins when pups are barely able to walk and continues into old age. Like children, dogs have favorite toys and will play with them until the toys literally fall apart.

behaviors make it likely that you will see your own dog, or the dog across the street, reflected in the following pages.

Some of the best things about dogs are the company, friendship, and protection they offer. Companionship and protection toward an owner are foremost on every dog's mind. That's why so many of us spend time talking to our dogs. Who better to share our secrets, joys, and sorrows? Dogs can't talk, but that doesn't mean they don't have plenty to say—to each other, to other animals, and to us, their beloved humans. They want to see their owner laugh, and they want to safeguard their favorite people from danger. Dogs will lay down their life for their owner. We should have human friends so devoted!

Knowing this, it's easy to see why dogs serve people so zealously and are so eager to be of help to us. Such admirable characteristics are an integral part of the canine mind, heart, and spirit. The dog just can't help being a friend, and fortunate is the man, woman, or child who discovers this.

Dogs are our silent counselors, our sounding boards, and our best pals (left).

If you pick up a starving dog and make him prosperous, he will not bite you. This is the principal difference between a dog and a man.
—*Mark Twain*

One of the best things about dogs is that they can share many of our interests. Because dogs were bred for so many different purposes, there is a breed that's just right for whatever it is we want to do—from playing catch on the beach to pulling a sled through snow-covered fields. There are dogs who are best for stretching out beside us on the sofa and watching football, and there are dogs who are best for going outside with us and playing football. Which breed is best for you?

DOG TAILS

Dogs laugh, but they laugh with their tails.

—*Max Eastman*

Communication is essential among dogs, just as it is essential among people. Dogs speak up loud and clear through body posture, with the wagging tail the best known (and loved!) of all the dog's signs. To owners, an upright, wagging tail indicates a friendly, happy pet. It's a welcome sight, one that says, "I'm delighted to see you."

Most of us are familiar with this happy tail wag, but dogs can indicate many other emotions with a wag of the tail. How high the tail is held and how slow or fast it moves give clues to what a dog is saying. A tail tucked between the legs can indicate that a dog is fearful or submissive. A confident dog wags her tail

Dogs are brilliant students of human nature. They watch us carefully and tailor their behavior to our actions and body language. It's a rare dog who can't communicate what she wants, especially a dog advanced in years. This elderly Golden Retriever waits patiently for her owners to notice that she's ready to come inside.

We all have anxious moments, and the position of a dog's tail gives a good indication of how she is feeling. This Whippet (right) shows she is feeling nervous by tucking her tail between her legs. She may also be acting submissive toward another dog or a person. A bold, excited dog holds her tail high and proud, wagging it furiously.

high up in the air; a timid dog wags hesitantly. A loose, wide wag is a good indication of a submissive dog; an aggressive dog moves her tail in short, quick wags, if she even moves it at all.

In style, too, each tail wag is special. Most dogs have a characteristic wag. A Great Dane, with her long, whiplike tail, can clear a coffee table in one swipe. A Doberman Pinscher with a docked tail looks like she's dancing: Her hindquarters sway vigorously from side to side. The soft swish of an Irish Setter's feathered tail is reminiscent of a flag waving gently in the breeze. Some dogs wag furiously, others hesitantly. Each tail on each dog is different.

Money will buy a pretty good dog, but it won't buy the wag of his tail.

—Josh Billings

REIGNING DOGS

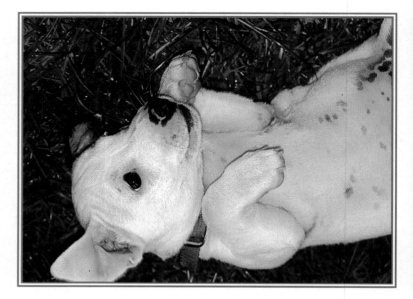

The tail is not the dog's only means of communication. Other forms of body language indicate a dog's place in the family, both in relation to other dogs and to people. Dogs have a distinct pecking order that helps everyone get along without fighting. Everyone has heard the term "top dog." Top dogs are the leaders in this pecking order, and all the other dogs in the household respect their place.

How do dogs know which one is the leader? Body postures tell all. Just like a winning politician or athlete, a top dog uses his personality and his looks to maintain his number-one spot in the house-

"I give up! You're the boss." This pup is displaying classic submissive behavior: lying on his back with his belly exposed. By making himself vulnerable, the dog is saying, "I don't want any trouble." That's just the message a dominant dog seeks before backing off and moving on to other business.

If a dog's prayers were answered, bones would rain from the sky.

—Anonymous

Unlike humans, dogs aren't shy about making their feelings known. They use distinct vocalizations and body language to get their point across. This canine language is learned early in puppyhood and is the reason why it is important for a pup to remain with her mother and littermates until seven or eight weeks of age. Below, a Border Collie expresses displeasure by snarling at an Alaskan Malamute.

hold. He makes himself look larger than life by standing tall and erect, with the hair on his back bristling, ears held high, tail up, and lips curled. His appearance sends a clear message to all other dogs: "I'm the boss!" A lower-ranking dog with any sense

expresses agreement by making himself look smaller. He may crouch, lay his head on his paws, and lower his ears. Just to make sure the top dog gets the message, the submissive dog may roll onto his back with his paws up. These actions all say "You're the boss."

Since dogs can't speak, they must rely heavily on body language to understand each other. This Akita is displaying a classic submissive position by crouching with his head down. He may be expressing deference to an older dog or to his beloved human.

DOG PLAY

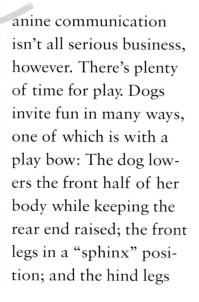

Canine communication isn't all serious business, however. There's plenty of time for play. Dogs invite fun in many ways, one of which is with a play bow: The dog lowers the front half of her body while keeping the rear end raised; the front legs in a "sphinx" position; and the hind legs stretched. The playful dog stares at her potential playmate and makes small, quick, forward movements as if to say, "Come on! Let's play!" When your dog does this, give a play bow back and then start a fun game of fetch or whatever your dog likes to do.

In addition to using body language to express such emotions as pleasure or anger, dogs also use it to indicate a desire to play. This dog is exhibiting what is called a "play bow"—a clear message that he feels playful and is ready for a game.

What a ham! This Pomeranian knows her smiling face is irresistible. Other dogs gazing at this small dog would smile, too, because in dog language a smile is a subtle invitation for fun.

Another, more subtle play invitation is a smile. Have you ever seen your dog's lips pulled back horizontally, with the jaws slightly opened? In the animal kingdom, just as with people, this expression means that no harm is intended. A dog's smile is heartwarming to see,

and indeed few owners can help smiling back.

Dogs also express their desire to play by nudging, pawing, and dancing. A playful dog may sit before her companion, stare, then make downward motions with one front paw. Some dogs are relentless, nudging and pawing an owner until the games begin. For some dogs, the spirit of play is more than they can bear. Don't expect a simple play bow from these dogs! They will prance, whirl, twist, and leap to express their desire for fun. Their entire bodies get in on the action, from the nose to the tip of the tail. It's hard to mistake such exuberance for anything but play.

Who can resist such a happy dog? This Afghan Hound (left) dances exuberantly, her luxurious coat swirling around her. Everything a dog thinks and feels is translated through body language. When a dog is excited, as this Afghan obviously is, you'll know it. Conversely, if she's feeling blue, her sad expression and lethargic behavior will give her away.

Some dogs show more teeth than others when they smile. This dog has what is called an undershot jaw, meaning that his lower jaw sticks out farther than his upper jaw, giving him an unusual look. In most dogs, such a bite is not desirable, though in some breeds such as the Bulldog or Shih Tzu it is considered fashionable. Every dog's face is special because it expresses the love within.

Our dogs are endlessly willing to join in a mutually pleasing arrangement. He or she will do his or her part to be faithful, loyal, loving, to listen and pay attention. I hope as much can be said for us.

—Roger Caras

Who can resist this smiling face? Yes, dogs do smile—and when they do, they express a playful heart. You'd never guess by looking at this Staffordshire Bull Terrier's sweet, happy expression that the breed was originally bred for bull-baiting, a bloody sport in which animals were pitted against each other for "entertainment." Fortunately, that horrid sport came to an end in the 1800s. Now that's something dogs and animal lovers can smile about!

DOG TALK

Body language is not the only way dogs tell us how they feel. Sound plays a big role, too. Dogs communicate through a variety of vocalizations, including barks, howls, growls, whimpers, and whines. The only dog who doesn't bark is the Basenji, a hound from Africa. Basenjis are far from silent, however. They yodel and yip, and fans of this breed claim they even talk!

Barking is the canine version of an alarm system. It is meant to alert members of the family, canine or human, to anything out of the ordinary. In the wild, the sound of barking causes pups to dash for safety and adults to prepare for action. The volume and type of barking usually correspond to the intensity of the message. For example, a dog may emit a sharp, staccato bark when a stranger knocks at the door but will let loose an exuberant bark when his favorite person returns

A dog can express more with his tail in minutes than his owner can express with his tongue in hours.

—Anonymous

You won't hear any barking from this pair of Basenjis (opposite page), but that doesn't mean they are silent. This breed, discovered by Westerners about 100 years ago in Central Africa, yodels to make its presence known. In addition to their unique vocalizations, Basenjis have another interesting characteristic: their gait, which is a swift, tireless trot.

The aggressive threats of this Doberman Pinscher (above) must be taken seriously. While Dobermans are highly intelligent companions and friends, they are also fierce guards and are frequently trained as such. All dogs have the potential to show aggression, though certain breeds have more of what it takes to back it up.

bark is worse than his bite," is based on a canine truth. A barking dog is usually feeling some amount of fear or apprehension; a truly aggressive dog is fearless and doesn't utter a sound. The dog who barks is usually not brave enough to bite, but the dog who bites

home. An astute owner learns how to decipher her dog's barks to determine meaning, much like a mother learns to understand the cries of her baby.

Just like a tail wag, a bark can be friendly, or it can serve as a warning. The saying "His

There's no mistaking this dog's mood (below): He's highly agitated and may attack. Aggressive signals such as barking, growling, bared teeth, and snapping are designed to intimidate. There are differing types of aggressive displays, and dogs use them for many reasons, including competition for food, mates, pack dominance, or territory.

doesn't bother to sound an alarm. Snarling and growling indicate aggression, so it is wise to approach cautiously when a dog is behaving this way. A snarling dog is warning that an attack may follow.

The same way a growl or snarl indicates that a dog is having a bad fur day, a howl serves as a kind of long-distance beeper service. It's as though the dog is saying, "I'm here, where are you?" One howling dog soon may be accompanied by a concert of neighborhood dogs. Howling is also associated with sexuality. Males separated from females in season will howl; the females will answer in kind.

Born to pull a sled through the snow and ice in subzero weather, this Siberian Husky (left) takes a moment to call his comrades. Howling is the dog's way of calling the pack—in this case, the sled team. Unlike some other breeds that bark more than they howl, Siberian Huskies (like most Nordic breeds) howl more than they bark. In addition to howling for company, dogs—especially hounds—may howl when they have located prey or in response to another dog's howl. Even the sound of an ambulance siren can elicit a howl.

NOSING AROUND

Body language and sound are how people understand what our dogs are telling us, but when it comes to scent, dogs have us beat by a long shot. There's no way we can appreciate all the nuances a dog picks up just by using her nose.

Dogs spend a good part of their time sniffing, thanks to an extremely well-developed sense of smell. The sense of smell is so well developed, in fact, that Bloodhounds can follow a trail four days old and track a human up to 100 miles. Sniffing isn't just for fun, however. Dogs communicate to each other through odor. This is why when two unfamiliar

Smell shouts to dogs, whose noses are so keen they can sniff out items undetectable to people. Smell also tells a dog how tasty a meal might be, which is why dogs smell food before eating.

dogs meet, they begin sniffing each other nose to nose, then smell each other's bodies head to tail. Smell helps dogs communicate territorial messages, convey sexual readiness, and confirm identity, among other things.

When two dogs meet, the first order of business is to get to know each other. While the idea may seem uncivilized, even undignified, to humans, there are few pleasures more enjoyable to dogs than a good whiff.

40 WINKS

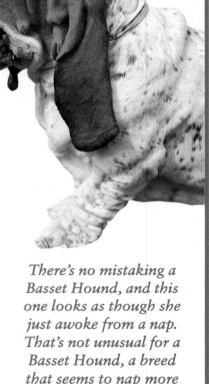

There's no mistaking a Basset Hound, and this one looks as though she just awoke from a nap. That's not unusual for a Basset Hound, a breed that seems to nap more than any other. Or at least they get caught napping quite often. A big yawn and stretch will get this hound moving, probably off to find a snack.

Dogs are very particular in their sleeping habits. Sometimes they turn around three times before lying down, a ritual that is left over from the dog's wild ancestry, when they needed to prepare the earth to be a comfortable resting place. And where a dog sleeps is very important. A dog may have his very own bed, but that doesn't mean he will sleep in it. A dog's favorite sleeping spot is almost always right next to his owner, and he will go to extraordinary measures to make sure he sleeps by his owner's side. Some people think this is wonderful; others, especially people who own a large Saint Bernard or an especially rambunctious Boston Terrier, would just as soon have their dog sleep right beside them—on the floor!

Although we tend to think of them as always on the go, dogs enjoy a good snooze as much as anyone. Unlike humans, they rarely have trouble sleeping and often adapt their schedule to that of their owners, resting during the day and spending time with their people in the evening. At night, they settle down next to or even on the bed, ready to catch a few more winks. The sight and scent of a beloved human ensures that they get a good night's sleep.

INSTINCTUAL BEHAVIOR

Digging is a favorite canine activity. The flying dirt provides entertainment, and the resulting hole can be a good hiding place for a bone or a cool bed in which to escape summer's heat. Nordic breeds such as the Samoyed enjoy digging, even though it is unlikely that today's incarnation would need to scrape out a cozy nest in the snow the way their ancestors once did. This Samoyed looks as if she's trying to dig all the way to China.

Tail wagging, barking, howling, and sniffing are fairly common behaviors that are familiar to most dog owners, but sometimes dogs do things that seem just plain strange to us. But once we understand how the dog's brain works, these actions make perfect sense.

For instance, why on earth might a dog bury a bone? And why do they always bury a newly purchased (and expensive) rawhide chew? It's simple. When there's a surplus of food, as there is for most domestic dogs, instinct prompts the dog to bury any food she can't eat at the moment. This behavior is seen in wolves and wild dogs. A rawhide chew is surplus

Talk about a refined act! This pair of longhaired Dachshunds have perfected the art of begging. Though it's not a behavior to be encouraged because it can injure the Dachshund's long back, begging is definitely cute.

familiaris tradition, and it requires little effort from the dog aside from a pitiful expression that says "I'm starving. I haven't eaten for days." Some dogs have perfected the trick, and these performers will raise themselves up on their hind legs just in case you don't notice them down there by your feet. Dogs beg because human food smells are irresistible—and because they quickly learn that owners give in.

food to the dog's mind; therefore, it must be saved for later.

Another common dog behavior—one that's not so strange—is begging. Begging is a *canis*

Dogs are natural-born show-offs, especially the terriers, who love to be the center of attention whenever possible. When a dog is this anxious to please a crowd, it's easy to teach him tricks. This West Highland White Terrier has obviously been taught to beg on command, which is a good way to keep begging behavior under control.

Begging is just one of the ways in which dogs have learned to live successfully with people. It and other behaviors beg the question: Are dogs intel-

Manners make the dog! A dog who knows and obeys simple commands is a pleasure to be around. For most dogs, learning a few basic commands is quick business, and it is an important part of socialization.

ligent, or do they do what they do simply as a result of instinct? To be sure, the dog's inborn pack mindset results in instinctual behaviors—behaviors that dogs do naturally without real thought. But dogs do have a form of intelligence that is beyond instinct, a fact that is evident to most any dog owner. (Don't mention this to cat owners, but dogs have higher IQs than the feline species.) Dogs are smart, keen companions, some-

times sharper than their owners. Or at least it seems that way when dog outsmarts owner!

Dogs are excellent learners. They can make associations between ideas and, as a result, perform tasks such as following a simple command. They understand subtle cues from humans, just as they understand body language from each other. For example, a dog can learn that a simple wave of the hand means sit or a nod of the head means lie down. They also pick up on

This German Shepherd Dog illustrates the alert intensity with which the breed approaches life. The German Shepherd's keen wit and ability to focus are what enable him to excel in obedience competition—and anything else he chooses to do. High-level obedience training is challenging. It requires good communication between dog and trainer and—more important—a dog who is eager to learn.

This Bichon Frise stands alert, attentive, and ready, a perfect state for learning. Dogs are highly intelligent and benefit greatly from the mental and physical rigors of obedience training. In fact, some dogs need the mental challenge of formal training in order to keep out of trouble. All dogs, regardless of their size, shape, or personality, can learn, though they may have differing aptitudes. Those differences are what makes each breed and individual dog unique.

No one knows better than a dog how to make his owner feel more important than he is.

—*Stephen Baker*

less direct signals, such as recognizing that when their owner puts on a pair of gym shoes, it may be time for a walk.

Are all dogs equally intelligent? That depends on what you want the dog to do. Certain breeds show different aptitudes. For example, a herding dog would probably ignore a fallen duck. By the same token, a retriever would most likely be stymied by a flock of sheep. Does this mean either dog lacks intelligence? No, each is simply better suited—physically and mentally—for a different job.

A well-educated, loved, and socialized dog will learn quickly to commu-

nicate her ideas. Training and attention help dogs develop memory and experience, which they use to associate ideas. Associating a leash with going for a walk is one idea that dogs pick up quickly— perhaps because it means fun! A dog who wants to take a stroll will bring the leash to her owner. That dog has learned to associate a leash with her desire to go out—and no self-respecting owner should refuse such a well-thought-out plan.

Dogs are truly fun, interesting, and helpful companions. There is little a devoted dog won't do for her owner. But, hey, what are friends for?

Each dog has special talents and abilities, but there's one thing that all dogs are good at: turning those big, sad eyes on us and using them to get walks, food, and petting. As long as dogs know how to do that, their intelligence will never be in doubt (opposite page).

Chapter 5

Having Fun Together

*I think we are drawn to dogs because
they are the uninhibited creatures we might be
if we weren't certain we knew better.*

—George Bird Evans

THE HUMAN–ANIMAL BOND

Previous page: These carefree dogs frolic at water's edge.

O ne of the wonderful gifts dogs bring to their relationship with people is a profound feeling of contentment and peace. An activity as simple as stroking a pet can cause our bodies to relax and our blood pressure to drop. The special feeling evoked by the attachment to a dog is called the human–animal bond, and it is undoubtedly beneficial to the physical and emotional well-being of people.

That conclusion is not news to dog owners. Befriending a dog is a rewarding experience, one that few owners regret. It's also a lot of fun. Besides a feeling of devotion and dedication to its owner, the canine heart is filled with a need to play—a need to

Warm weather is a great time to get the entire family in on bathing the dog. Hook up a hose, grab the shampoo, and start scrubbing. Don't wear your Sunday best, though. Dog bathing is a messy affair. Parents, beware of young children and dogs at bathtime. They're apt to join forces and turn the hose on you!

The greatest pleasure of a dog is that you may make a fool of yourself with him, and not only will he not scold you, but he will make a fool of himself too.

—Samuel Butler

Dogs love to be photographed, and, like this smiling hound, will make sure they're front and center of every snapshot.

have fun. Play begins in puppyhood as playmates romp and scramble. It continues throughout the dog's entire life; even an old, tired dog with arthritis can be coaxed into a short game or activity. Having fun together is the basis of a good owner–dog relationship. And the sky's the limit as to what owners and dogs can find to do together for fun.

EXERCISE

Perhaps the most popular activity people enjoy with their dog is strolling throughout the neighborhood together. Sometimes a walk is a necessity when nature calls, sometimes it's undertaken to get some exercise, and sometimes people walk just to relax. Whatever the reason, a walk is a simple but fulfilling activity for both owner and dog.

For the early riser, a morning walk is a great way to spend time with a canine friend. The air is fresh, and the day is just beginning to unfold. Since most dogs are early risers, there's usually no argument about getting out of bed. Some owners prefer evening strolls, wandering about just as the sun sets. Dogs enjoy it, too: It's the perfect end to a day.

Dashing through the leaves...what better way to celebrate fall than to run through a leaf pile? Few dogs can resist the scent and sound of a pile of leaves, and dogs who love the great outdoors are sure to derive maximum enjoyment from this novel activity.

A dog is one of the few remaining reasons why some people can be persuaded to go for a walk.

—*O.A. Battista*

Whether walking through flowery fields or along a wooded path, dogs are constant companions to people. They seem to enjoy the sights as much as we do (right).

A dog is a great workout companion for fitness walkers; those owners who walk briskly to burn calories, lose weight, and increase muscle tone. Just like their owners, canine fitness walkers must gradually build up strength. Otherwise, it means sore muscles or perhaps even an injury—just the same as for humans who begin a fitness program. Once a dog is fit, though, owners will have a tough time keeping up! Once a dog learns to associate the sight of a leash with the prospect of heading out for a walk, owners had best prepare themselves for unbridled enthusiasm, including jumps, lunges, and yelps, at the very sight of the leash.

Jogging is another activity adored by most dogs. While it's not appropriate for every dog or owner, jogging together builds a feeling of camaraderie, as well as building up health and well-being. A dog can also be a safeguard for a lone jogger who may feel unsafe. A jog through the park or a run at the sea's edge is invigorating, often essential, for the high-energy dog. Just like their owners, dogs get "hooked" on running, living for the next moment when the leash and jogging shoes appear. For dogs, jogging with an owner is much more than an activity. It's spending time with their favorite person!

Running may be an individual sport, but it's certainly never lonely when you bring a canine friend along. This Golden Retriever (left) knows the route so well she doesn't need a leash, and the area is so quiet there's no traffic danger. In fact, it looks as though she's leading the way and setting the pace. Let's hope she's a merciful coach!

This dog and owner combine two popular activities: cycling and running. Together, they enjoy exercise and have fun. The dog who is able to keep up with a conditioned cyclist is quite an athlete himself. Consistent exercise, nutritious meals, and plenty of rest are vital to all athletes, and dogs are no exception.

Some people enjoy bicycling or roller-skating while their dog jogs beside them. The quick pace is no problem for a fit and nimble canine athlete—and it's a great way to burn off steam for human high achievers. It's also fun to watch a coordinated team cruising along, like poetry in motion. Creative dog owners will find any number of athletic activities to enjoy with their canine companions.

WATER SPORTS

Some dogs are natural-born swimmers, and if they're fortunate, they live with owners who share their passion for getting wet. Breeds such as the Golden Retriever and Labrador Retriever are happiest near water: They are thrilled by romping in a lake or an ocean, riding in a boat, playing with children in the backyard swimming pool, or even just cooling off in a creek. Though some breeds take to water more naturally than others, all dogs and owners can share the excitement of water sports. It's just a matter of getting their feet wet, so to speak.

What's better than one swimming Golden Retriever? Two swimming Golden Retrievers, of course. If this breed wasn't a member of the canine species, you'd think it was related to the duck. Goldens are powerful swimmers who love water activities of any kind, especially those coupled with a retrieval task.

Whether alone or with friends, this dog knows there's nothing like playing in the surf. The constant ebbs and flows are a mystery to the canine mind, which makes it all the more fun. Water comes in, water goes out. When the water goes out, there are all kinds of creatures to chase and all sorts of scents to smell. And when the water comes in, it's delightful to run and splash in the waves.

Ta da! Not only are dogs great swimmers, but they're great divers, too. It doesn't take much to motivate a dog to dive in, either. Toss a ball or favorite toy and—splash! Though water entry certainly wouldn't earn this canine diver points in competition, his style and concentration are outstanding.

"Splish, splash, I was taking a bath."
*And from the looks of this dog's
enthusiastic shaking, whoever gave her
the bath is just as wet as she is! Some
dogs accept bathtime quite gracefully,
but others are convinced they must share
the wet, soapy festivities with their
favorite two-legged friend. Owners
should keep in mind that this good, clean
fun is meant in the spirit of play.*

*For some dogs, there's nothing like getting wet. And if the body of water
is a river, that's even better. With miles of shore to explore, a dog can
spend hours splashing, running, sniffing, and swimming. It may be best
not to take a water-loving dog fishing, though. He simply won't be able
to sit quietly on shore waiting for a bite!*

*There are three faithful
friends—an old wife, an old
dog, and ready money.*
—Benjamin Franklin

HORSING AROUND

*F*or many people, the love of animals isn't limited to dogs. Dog owners are frequently horse owners, which means that dog and horse usually meet. In fact, most owners wouldn't think of taking a trip to the stable or going for a ride without their canine companion. A horse–rider–dog trio is usually a good mix, once the dog learns barn and trail etiquette (don't bark at the horses, get too close to their feet, eat manure, or chew leather equipment) and the horse learns dog etiquette (don't step on the dog!). Trail riding can be delightful, but it's even more fun when a dog tags along.

Dogs and horses have worked together for centuries. Dalmatians (below) frequently are kept in stables because riders know that these dogs won't spook their horses. The heritage of Jack Russell Terriers (opposite page) is linked to horses as well. Jack Russells were carried on horseback in small sacks and were released to unearth quarry from its lair during the hunt.

OUTDOOR ACTIVITIES

If dogs were polled, camping and hiking would probably be voted "Number One Best Sport." Dogs are excellent campers—they prefer not to bathe for days at a time and don't mind sleeping on the ground, "roughing it," or getting dirty. To the canine mind, the great outdoors—with its myriad smells, wild animals, and places to explore— is heaven. A good day of hiking through a forest (one that permits pets) will a happy dog make. And sleeping under the stars next to a roaring fire is nothing less than the perfect end to any dog's exhausting day of exploration and discovery.

What camping trip is complete without the family dog? Check first to make sure the park accepts pets, then pack up Rover's sleeping pad, dog food, collar and leash, and food bowls. The rest of the trip is sure to be memorable because wherever dogs go, so does fun.

of a romp with his best pal? In some communities, there are even parks created just for dogs. These parks, sometimes called "Bark Parks," are fenced areas or safe places in which a dog can run off leash. This is a real treat—especially for city dogs who may not be not used to such freedom and spontaneity.

As if catching a Frisbee flying disc weren't difficult enough with two hands: How about trying to catch one with your mouth? To dogs, it's all in a day's work—or more accurately, a day's fun. Tossing a Frisbee for Fido has progressed from a simple owner–dog activity to a highly competitive sport. Canine Frisbee competitions, which take place all over the U.S., are awesome to watch.

What some dogs lack in size, they make up for in determination. Chasing after a ball is a favorite occupation for some dogs; they will go after it as long as their owner keeps tossing it.

Picnics in the park are just the place for canine family members. Families enjoy the dogs, and the dogs enjoy the good food. Parks are a great place for games of fetch, and what dog isn't excited by the prospect

WORK IS NOT A FOUR–LETTER WORD

*T*o the canine mind, fun and work are synonymous. This can be difficult for owners to understand; most believe work and fun are separate. Work is something that has to be done in order to earn money, for example. Fun comes later, after chores are finished. But dogs think differently—and to understand that, we look to the canine domestication process. As dogs were domesticated throughout the ages, they were often bred for specific tasks. The work for which a breed was designed is more than the dog's job—it's who the dog is. The inborn aptitudes for a task come forth naturally, joyfully, and without much effort. The dog's work isn't really work. It's sport.

Though Greyhound racing is a controversial sport, there's no doubt that the breed is fast and well-suited for the activity. Once retired from the track, Greyhounds make excellent pets and devoted companions. They are playful, intelligent friends who are especially fun to take for a walk. Because most people associate Greyhounds with the racetrack, seeing one walking through the neighborhood can be an unexpected treat.

The best-known dogsled race—the Iditarod— takes place every March in Alaska. Teams race some 1,000 miles through difficult conditions. The annual race commemorates the dogsled relay teams used to rush diphtheria serum from Anchorage to Nome to stop an epidemic in 1925.

Today, even though few dogs still do the work for which they were developed, many people and dogs still enjoy such dog sports as retrieving, herding, dogsledding, skijoring, and more. (Skijoring, in which the dog pulls a person on skis, is a hybrid of cross-country skiing and dogsledding, a sort of scaled-down version of mushing.) These activities give dogs a chance to show off their inborn talents.

"Live to herd!" is surely this Border Collie's motto. Farmers often consider livestock dogs their most important, and best, employees— and who wouldn't? These dogs love to work, don't complain, are never late, and never ask for a raise.

using ducks at events called herding tests, in which they round up the ducks and use their herding skills by moving them into a pen.

The furry dogs of the far North can participate in two exciting sports: dogsledding and skijoring. Dogsledding, also called mushing,

Hunting dogs display their prowess in events called field trials. There are different field trials for each type of hunting dog, such as Beagles, Basset Hounds, pointing dogs, spaniels, retrievers, and Dachshunds. And even though most people nowadays don't own flocks of sheep or cattle, herding dogs can demonstrate their skill

It's said that a Corgi's work is never done, and this Pembroke Welsh Corgi proves the point by trying to gather up an uncooperative foursome of ducks. Even though as a breed Corgis are quite short, they are excellent working and herding dogs. The Corgi has been a favorite breed of the working class and royalty alike: Britain's Queen Elizabeth owns several and is seldom seen taking a stroll without them.

Life on the Iditarod trail is challenging—and the ability to finish the race depends on teamwork. The musher must nurture and feed a team of hungry dogs in subzero temperatures. In turn, the dogs follow commands, move quickly, and get along with each other. The hard work is enjoyable for the dogs.

capitalizes on the natural talents of Northern breeds such as Alaskan Malamutes, Samoyeds, and Siberian and Alaskan Huskies. These dogs are hearty, thrive in the cold, and love to run. Therefore, dogsledding is a special treat for them! Even if you don't live in an area with lots of snow, with the right equipment, you and your dog can still enjoy the thrill of these sports by training the dog to pull you in a wheeled vehicle.

If you and your dog aren't very athletic but would still like to participate in a sport, obedience trials or conformation shows might be for you. In obedience showing, a dog learns specific tasks and must perform them precisely. All dogs should learn basic obedience com-

Just as brightly colored tropical fish are at home in the Caribbean, the Siberian Husky and other northern breeds are at home in low temperatures and snow. In fact, life just wouldn't be quite right without a snowy field in which to romp. This happy canine shows his appreciation of the white stuff by barking and running as fast as he can.

mands, but formal obedience training and showing have special rewards for both dog and owner. The dog who completes these tasks successfully can earn beginning to advanced titles. A variation of obedience trials

This handsome Golden Retriever clears a jump with seemingly little effort during an obedience competition. Obedience trials are a great opportunity for dogs to show off their skills, and they're a lot of fun, too. Preparing for a show is hard work for dog and trainer, but you'd never know it by the happy look on this dog's face.

Old dogs, like old shoes, are comfortable. They might be a bit out of shape and a little worn around the edges, but they fit well.

—Bonnie Wilcox and Chris Walkowicz

is called freestyle, in which dog and owner perform a routine set to music. Just think what you and your dog could do with the tunes "You Ain't Nothin' But a Hound Dog" or "How Much is that Doggie in the Window?"

Conformation shows evaluate a dog's appearance and soundness and can be a fun activity for the family that enjoys travel, meeting new people, and, of course, grooming and spending time with their dog. Children as young as nine years old can show their dogs, and often the whole family gets involved.

This champion Beagle stands attentively in the show ring as she waits to be examined. Show dogs must stand obediently while the judge looks them over from nose to tail. This 13-inch Beagle displays the keenness and coloration—right down to her white-tipped tail—for which the breed is known.

Though it hardly can be said that the canine species is one to rest on its laurels, being a show champion comes easily to some dogs, like this Samoyed. As they say, when you've got it, you've got it!

HANGING OUT

The more laid-back dog owner need not feel left out. Sports are fun, but most dogs are happy just to hang out with their people, any time, any place. A common sight on both city and country roads is a dog's head hanging out a car window, ears flapping, tongue hanging out, and what looks to be a grin of pure pleasure plastered across the dog's mug. Some owners relax by taking Fido for a leisurely drive, destination nowhere. Other people just enjoy their dog's company and choose to bring their buddy along on errands or wherever it is they need to go. And you can be sure that most dogs

There's nothing like taking in the sights while traveling, and this German Shepherd Dog is doing just that during a rest stop. While it's never a good idea to let a dog ride with her head out a window, it is a good idea to open the window for fresh air during a break. Some dogs enjoy riding so much that the sound of jangling car keys will send them racing to the front door.

Is it really true that blondes have more fun? Absolutely, according to this big golden dog. After all, who wouldn't want to take a spin in a convertible sports car with his best friend on a gorgeous day?

don't object! The exciting sounds, sights, and smells rushing past are intriguing. Responsible owners will make sure the dog can't hurt himself or get into trouble—never leave the window open so far a dog may be tempted to jump out of the car to further explore. Cracking the window a few inches should satisfy the dog's urge to take in the smells along the way.

for example, were bred for the specific purpose of being a companion. Snuggling up next to their owner comes naturally to them. In fact, they live for it.

Dog lovers will agree: There's nothing quite like cuddling together on the

It's a tough job, but somebody has to do it! This apricot Toy Poodle stretches out on her couch for a morning nap. Dogs will frequently "take over" a piece of furniture in the house, and trouble will surely come to whoever tries to take it back. Probably wishing to keep the couch a bit cleaner, this dog's wise owner covered the sofa with a blanket.

No one knows when the first dogs sought out a human's fire. Why they did is a much simpler question to figure. A fire is warm and inviting, which makes it a cozy place by which to sleep. Not much has changed in all the years since dogs and people befriended each other. A dog still loves napping next to the fire and can rest there peacefully for hours.

Sometimes the best way to spend time with your dog pal is simply to spend time with him! Dogs, even the most high-spirited, active breeds, excel at relaxing and cuddling with their favorite people—some were even bred for it. Pugs,

Blessed is the person who has earned the love of an old dog.

—Sidney Jeanne Seward

couch or in an over-stuffed chair while watching television (no documentaries on cats, please) or reading. Simply sitting together enjoying each other's company is a great way to unwind after a hard day—or not so hard day—at work. No matter how bad a person feels when he or she arrives home, a few moments of relaxing with the dog can change that.

Of course, some dogs are too big to sit on the couch (they try to do so

anyway), so sitting at—or on!—their master's feet is an option. For Saint Bernards or Giant Schnauzers, this is the way to go!

Whatever you and your dog are doing, there's one activity you can always be assured all dogs will enjoy, and that's a nice tummy-

Good things come in large as well as small packages. But large packages, like this Great Dane, don't always fit on the couch! This handsome Great Dane obviously knows a good thing when he sees it, and he's determined to get comfortable anywhere he wants to. After all, a couch is a comfortable spot to relax, and dogs are smart enough to know that.

Surprisingly, this Border Collie brings only the newspaper, not the paperboy and a few neighborhood friends, to her master. This breed loves to herd—everything. Herding aside, many breeds, including the Border Collie, assist their owners by fetching the daily newspaper. Why do they do it? Some are trained. Others are just helpful!

rubbing, rib-patting, ear-scratching petting. It's pleasing to the dog, and most dogs live for a simple pat on the head. Scratch behind the ears, stroke the head and muzzle. Rub the dog's tummy, pat his ribs. Dogs can't resist such affection; they melt like butter. Petting the dog is also good for the owner. A few strokes, and blood pressure drops. The owner feels a sense of well-being and can almost feel tension and stress receding. Scientific studies prove all this, but there's no need to analyze data. The proof is—and always has been—in the petting!

Fidelity and sincerity are the companion dog's greatest virtues and when reciprocated can be a wonderful bonus.

—Kay White

Few things in life are more restful than relaxing with a good book and a canine friend nearby. This scene of contentment isn't unusual. In fact, it's commonplace to dog owners, who enjoy such simple pleasures daily. That is part of the wonder of owning a dog.

Chapter 6

Special Assistants

Dogs are the only creatures
gifted to serve us beyond the
call of duty.

—C.W. Meisterfeld

INVALUABLE HELPERS

Previous page: Labrador Retrievers and Golden Retrievers make wonderful service dogs.

Those of us who have experienced the unconditional love of a dog know why dogs are called man's best friend, but the cords entwining the hearts of dogs and people are woven even more tightly by the shared workloads they shoulder. Together, people and dogs have hunted for food, cared for flocks, and guarded loved ones. But as is their nature, dogs have gone the extra mile for us. They have learned to help people who need physical or emotional support. Called service dogs, these dogs open up new lifestyles for people who might otherwise be unable to live independently.

The challenges associated with raising children are intensified when one or both parents is physically challenged. Everyday activities often taken for granted can be difficult. However, a service dog is helpful to the entire family. A guide dog helps this woman walk her children to and from school just like any other parent.

The close relationship between this man and his canine guide is based on trust. Traveling through a city, for example, requires an individual to rely on the dog's judgment of safe and unsafe conditions. Because of this, great care is taken by trainers to match the right dog with the right person. The pair must "click": The individual must feel comfortable with the dog and vice versa. Picking the right partner means the difference between success and failure.

Service dogs assist people who cannot see or hear, people who cannot walk, and people who suffer from seizures. Each dog is tailored to the needs of his person, and learns specific tasks—such as alerting his owner to the sound of the doorbell or turning on or off a light switch—to fill these needs.

SERVICE DOGS

Morris Frank, Dorothy Harrison Eustis, and Buddy in 1936. Eustis's dedication to the breed prompted her to begin breeding German Shepherd Dogs. Her dogs, known as the ultimate German Shepherds, were beautiful and very well trained.

Perhaps the most well-known service dogs are guide dogs. The history of guide dogs can be traced to Morris Frank, a young man from Nashville, Tennessee, who was blinded in two separate childhood accidents. Frank was highly motivated to live a normal life even though he was blind. This was unusual in the United States in the 1920s: People with disabilities either lived in institutions or lived out their days at home. Frank connected with Dorothy Harrison Eustis, a wealthy German Shepherd Dog enthusiast who had learned of German dogs trained to help disabled veterans. Frank convinced Eustis to train a

This German Shepherd guide-to-be proudly wears her training uniform. All service dogs wear uniforms that identify them as special assistants, which enables them to enter businesses, airports, shopping malls, or restaurants that normally do not allow dogs. Uniforms vary depending upon what type of assistant the dog is and which organization trained the dog.

dog for him—Buddy, a female German Shepherd originally named Kiss.

The match between Buddy and Frank was a success. Frank was so impressed he made it his life's work to enlist public interest and support for canine guides. In time, he was able to establish public recognition of the widespread

need for these special helpers as well as acceptance of dogs as aides for humans. In 1929, Frank and Eustis started a school called The Seeing Eye, Inc., which has since placed some 12,000 dogs. There are currently 1,800 graduates in North America.

Thanks to the help of these specially trained dogs, thousands of people with disabilities now enjoy greater independence. Activities such as walking to the grocery store, riding a bus downtown, or crossing a busy street can be possible with the help of a dog. Since the days of Morris Frank and Buddy, the idea of dogs helping people has spread like wildfire.

Dogs are directly beneficial to humans in a number of ways. Anyone who shares life with a dog knows how much affection, happiness, security, and warmth the dog gives. Indeed, the dog positively gives a lift to life.

—Judith Hancock

Service dogs—once rare—are now commonplace. There are numerous organizations that train dogs to assist the physically challenged. Most organizations are nonprofit and recipients do not pay for a canine helper, although some organizations do charge a nominal fee.

Initially, German Shepherds were most often chosen for this specialized training. Their intelligence, devotion, and agility make them excellent guides. Sadly, a defect called hip dysplasia made many of these dogs potentially unsound. A small percentage of German Shepherds are still chosen, but most organizations now train

Service dogs open up new opportunities for people. This Labrador Retriever assists a park employee with her daily duties in Rocky Mountain National Park (left). The desire to pursue a career in spite of physical difficulties is what originally motivated Morris Frank to seek out Mrs. Eustis and ask her to train a canine guide. While Frank did not have sight, he certainly had vision, a special gift that continues to benefit many individuals today.

foster families, where they learn the ins and outs of family life, then are returned to the school for intensive training at about 18 months of age. If the trained dogs meet school standards, they are then paired with a physically challenged individual.

This Samoyed performs a small, yet very helpful task: opening the door for his mistress. To someone who is physically challenged, opening a door can prove difficult. The help of a canine assistant can literally open doors to the world. Service dogs are trained for such tasks, but most dogs are helpful by nature and do not require much coaxing.

Service dogs, such as the German Wirehaired Pointer pictured here, are invaluable assistants to wheelchair-bound individuals. Not only does the dog help her master physically, but she also offers constant companionship and love. Such devotion and friendship are common to all dogs, but service dogs have unique opportunities to express these traits.

Golden Retrievers, Labrador Retrievers, or a mix of those breeds.

Training a dog to be a service companion is a hefty investment. One estimated cost of training a dog is $25,000. Most organizations either have their own private breeding programs or acquire pups from reputable breeders. Pups are placed with

WORKING DOGS

It looks as though these handsome, graceful English Setters have spotted some game. Though intent on their duties, the dogs appear gentle and kind. And they are. English Setters are sweet-natured in spite of their heart for hunting.

The career of service dog is fairly new in the annals of the dog–human relationship. It is only the latest in a long line of jobs that dogs have performed for people. The phrase "work like a dog" is used to describe working very hard, for a long period of time. And it comes pretty close to describing the canine work ethic. Dogs are hard workers and have been working companions to their masters for generations. Dogs herd sheep, guard property, rescue disaster victims, retrieve game, track people, and sniff out drugs for law enforcement officials. There are few jobs dogs cannot perform once they are adequately trained.

What an awesome sight this Chesapeake Bay Retriever is as she leaps into water in pursuit of game. Her form is perfect, her focus intense, and her desire to please overwhelming, which is why this breed is so appreciated. Close kin to the Labrador Retriever, the Chesapeake is a powerful swimmer and is happiest when soaking wet. There's no doubt this dog will bring back whatever her master has asked her to retrieve.

This Chesapeake Bay Retriever (below) soon will be asked by his hunter-master to hand over the game he's carried ever so carefully. While it looks like the dog has a tight grip on the bird, he actually carries it very gently so as not to cause any damage.

But not every dog is suited to every canine job. Certain breeds, due to natural talent and aptitude, are innately suited for particular jobs. Golden Retrievers, for example, excel at fetching game. Goldens don't have to be taught to carry something in their mouth; they do it naturally. At a mere eight weeks, a Golden pup is already carrying toys around in his mouth. In fact, Goldens are happiest when they are carrying something! Goldens also love water and are good swimmers. Of course, the dog must be taught the specifics of hunting, but the desire and ability to fetch downed game from a body of water is instinctive. Pointers—such as the German Shorthaired Pointer—are a hunter's companion, too, but instead of retrieving game, they point to it. This natural ability to signal—the dog stands

No, it's not a statue. It's a dog—a very still dog. This German Shorthaired Pointer is "on point," which means he's signaling to the hunter that game is nearby. Amazingly, pointing comes naturally to many breeds, though a hunter may teach a dog specific commands for use in the field. A well-trained pointer will remain still for a hour or more awaiting the next command.

In the United States and abroad, sheepdogs today assist farmers in their daily duties—as they have for generations. This man and his livestock dog inspect the German countryside for missing members of the flock. If one is found, a simple command sets the dog in motion to bring in the wanderer. Some sheepdogs live as family dogs, sharing the farmer's hearth. Others live year-round with the sheep, acting as protectors as well as herders.

rigid with one forepaw raised, nose in the wind, refusing to advance—is quite a sight to behold.

To be any good at looking after sheep, sheepdogs must be watchful, brave, gentle, and smart. High-strung or aggressive dogs are not right for the job. Several

breeds fit the job description, including the Border Collie and the Australian Kelpie. There are several different types of sheepdogs. The herder, for instance, brings strays back to the fold. The line dog protects crops by guiding on-the-move flocks around the crops instead

This scene may appear chaotic, but this Border Collie is sure to have the situation under control. Organizing and moving sheep and other livestock are what this breed lives to do. The Border Collie has been a favored herding dog and companion through the ages.

dogs serve in other ways. The canine instinct to guard and protect lends itself to another occupation: guard dog. Breeds such as the German Shepherd, Doberman Pinscher, and Giant Schnauzer, which are mighty in presence and fearless of heart, are commonly chosen for guard of through them. Another sheepdog stays by the farmer's side and intervenes on command. To a farmer, there's no substitute for a hard-working sheepdog.

In addition to their talents at hunting and herding, which are closely related activities,

It's not by chance a canine officer is leading this chase. With exceptional intelligence, a keen nose, and strength beyond compare, a dog is a talented member of a police team. Canine officers can track down, apprehend, and hold a suspect, often quicker than human officers. These highly trained dogs are intimidating to even the most hardened criminals—and should be! Off the job, police dogs aren't so fearsome. They often live with their partners as family pets.

Would you dare venture past this pair? The combination of this large snarling dog and large man in uniform creates a frightening picture of authority. Canine security guards quickly discourage would-be trespassers by barking, snapping, and growling.

the handcuffs. Many officers say that a canine partner is the best partner they've ever had, which isn't surprising given a dog's intelligence and devotion.

Property owners also benefit from the skills of a trained canine guard. A fierce-looking dog on patrol who can—and will—back up his bark is a great protector against crime. A prowler who meets a guard dog

This Dalmatian is one of many of her breed who call a fire station home and a firefighter master. Fire stations traditionally adopt a Dalmatian, who lives at the station and enjoys the special role of mascot. In the 1800s, American fire departments used Dalmatians—called Fire House Dogs by some—to coax and control the horses that pulled the fire equipment, which is how the breed became known as a fire station mascot.

training. Law enforcement agencies use guard dogs to help apprehend bad guys. A police officer's partner, for example, may be a dog trained to chase down and hold a bank robber until the officer slaps on

This Secret Service officer and his K-9 partner inspect a car for bombs. Using his incredible sense of smell, this dog sniffs for odors that could signal trouble. Dogs are able to smell things humans cannot. This dog may be able to determine in minutes if a bomb is present in the car; it would take a human hours, even days, to perform the same task.

face to face is unlikely to ever forget the encounter.

This is not to suggest that guard dogs are innately vicious. Guard dogs are highly trained and are taught specific actions such as to guard someone or something, to retrieve an object, or to attack. They are also taught not to take bribes! A dog on duty will not take a steak, no matter how tempting, from a would-be intruder. This is because bad-intentioned people have been known to hide harmful sub-

stances in foods a dog would normally find quite hard to resist.

Strength and agility are not the only assets of a working dog. Even small dogs such as Beagles make excellent canine employees. With their keen noses and fine intelligence, these dogs,

These Bloodhound pups have important jobs awaiting them. With a nose that can keep a scent for 100 miles, Bloodhounds are prized trackers who are highly valued by law enforcement officers. These youngsters may someday grow up to bring in an escaped felon, track down a missing child, or find a suspected criminal.

Can you imagine a more competent rescuer than a Saint Bernard (right)? Renowned for its ability to find and save people buried in the snow, the breed takes its name from the Hospice du Grand St. Bernard, located near the Italian border. The most successful Saint Bernard is said to have been a dog named Barry. He saved at least 40 lives before he died in 1814. The Saint Bernard is also said to have a sixth sense that enables him to predict avalanches.

as well as other breeds such as Labrador Retrievers, rapidly climb the corporate ladder as drug sniffers. Used by customs agents or local law enforcement, drug dogs sniff out hidden contraband. Dogs are so good at this that if any hint of drugs is present, the dog will find it.

The dog's keen nose can also be invaluable in rescuing victims of disasters. Search and rescue dogs can sniff out people caught in earthquake rubble or people buried under an avalanche. Saint Bernards are famous for their snow rescues. Contrary to popular images, real-life Saint Bernards on the job do not wear a keg of brandy around their

neck. Other breeds, such as the German Shepherd and the Bloodhound, are also well suited to finding victims.

THERAPY DOGS

*N*ot every dog works in food gathering, law enforcement, or rescue. Some dogs save lives in a very special way. Although they don't go to medical school (their knowledge is inborn), dogs perform important work in the health-care field, serv-ing as healers, coun-selors, and therapists.

The positive effect ani-mals have on people—lowering blood pressure, reducing stress, and cre-ating an overall feeling of well-being—has resulted in the growth of organizations dedicated to what is called animal-assisted therapy. For

Giving up a home due to illness and moving into a convalescent care center is difficult. Besides leaving a family home, it may mean giving up beloved pets. Nursing home residents who once owned pets especially appreciate regular visits by therapy dogs. This woman enjoys a few special moments holding and petting a sweet friend.

Humans have externalized their wisdom—stored it in museums, libraries, the expertise of the learned. Dog wisdom is inside the blood and bones.

—Donald McCaig

Did you know that laughter may not be the best medicine? Dogs may be! This darling dog may be the best medicine of all for some nursing home residents—a warm, attentive friend to hold and love.

instance, dogs have been used to help give severely depressed individuals a sense of responsibility and, thus, a reason for living. Therapists have long included pets in their work with abused children. Many therapists keep resident dogs in their office as counseling partners to comfort young patients. Dogs are wonderful friends and teachers to abused children. Kids who have been hurt and damaged by people usually feel safe befriending a dog. Dogs ask for nothing, other than a pat here or

Who says therapy dogs have to be lap size? This large fellow proves that dogs of any shape and size can become therapy dogs. What's most important is a sweet, loving disposition. To ensure therapy dogs are just that, the Delta Society—a nonprofit company based in Washington—developed Pet Partners, a certification program for therapy dogs and owners. Pet Partner dogs undergo skills and aptitude screening by a Delta Society evaluator, as well as a health exam by a veterinarian. Owners also must complete a Pet Partners training workshop.

there. They won't strike out or scream at the child. Kids are quick to understand this. Children who have been betrayed by adults learn that dogs truly can be their best friend!

Dogs visit hospitals and convalescent homes as ambassadors of healing, bringing a smile to many lonely faces. Not just any dog can be a therapy dog. While special training isn't required, a special sense is. Therapy dogs must be gentle, easy-going, and calm, with the ability to adjust quickly to

A man's dog stands by him in prosperity and poverty, in health and sickness. He will sleep on the cold ground, when the wintery winds blow and the snow drives fiercely, if only he can be near his master's side... When all other friends desert, he remains.

—*George Graham Vest*

new people and places. Any breed of dog can make a good therapy dog, as long as she is sensitive to individual needs. She will know to sit quietly next to an elderly person who is timid with dogs. She will also know when to put her paws into someone's lap and ask to jump in. A dog who does this kind of work must pass a complete health and temperament screening test. This ensures that only the best-suited dogs get a therapy job.

A typical therapy dog's visit to a nursing home or hospital is informal and much like a visit from anybody else— only better. A dog will wag her tail, smile, and wait to be petted. People who are ill or very lonely often light up when they see a dog. A dog is like a living photo album, bringing back memories of special dogs and good times in the past.

It's no wonder dogs are called man's best friend. Without their loving attitudes, hard work, and emotional sensitivity, we would be poor indeed.

Chapter 7

Myth, Lore, and Legends

You think dogs will not be in heaven?
I tell you, they will be there long before any of us.

—Robert Louis Stevenson

HOLY DOGS

Today, we view dogs primarily as our best friends. Throughout history, however, dogs have held sacred places in many cultures. Dogs have been represented in writings, pictographs, and stories that provide numerous insights and clues to the dog's place in past society.

Previous page: Greek terra-cotta figurine (circa 575 B.C.).

Dogs have been held in high esteem by many cultures and religions, but they weren't necessarily themselves the object of worship. Instead, a cult might have believed that gods manifested themselves through dogs. The dog became a representative of a god or was closely associated with the god.

Ancient Egypt wholeheartedly welcomed the

The scene on this gold flabellum (circa 1530 B.C.) depicts a Pharaoh hunting ostriches with Greyhounds. The Greyhound, in its modern form, was developed in Great Britain, but some historians believe that the breed's ancestors may have come from Mesopotamia or Ethiopia. Depictions of this breed are frequently found in Egyptian engravings and sculptures.

The Egyptians revered several kinds of animals, including the dog, which became the symbol of Anubis, god of the dead. In ancient Egypt, this god presided over the embalming of the dead. Like many of its time, this wooden Egyptian casket (1085–950 B.C.) is illustrated with a colorful scene. Anubis, the dog-headed man, is pictured second from the left.

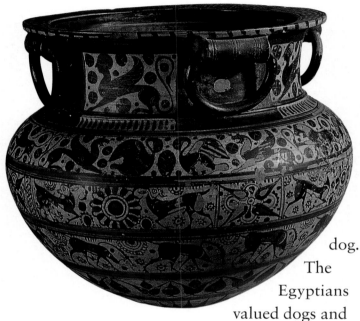

The Greeks' fondness for the dog is evidenced by the canine's appearance in myths, literature, and artwork. This handsome Greek pottery dates to the Orientalising period (615 B.C.). Stylized images of dogs were common in classical Greek art, especially in pottery and sculptures.

dog. The Egyptians valued dogs and recognized their importance as hunters. The dog, along with the falcon, ox, and cat, was endowed with a godlike status. According to legend, Horus, the great god of the Nile (the source of all life, according to ancient Egyptians), had four sons, including two with dog characteristics: dog-headed Hapi and jackal-headed Tuamautef. The four sons helped guide the deceased through the afterlife. This helps explain why the dog was a symbol of Anubis, god of the dead, who also guided human souls into the afterlife. Statues and drawings of Anubis depict him as having a human body and a dog-like or wolflike head.

Another god recognized by the Egyptians—Seth, the god of evil—was also manifested in the form of a dog. This god, as depicted in Egyptian artwork, looked like a Greyhound with erect ears and a forked tail. From this, breed historians have suggested that Egypt is the home of the modern Greyhound. Despite this association

Heaven goes by favor. If it went by merit, you would stay out and your dog would go in.
—*Mark Twain*

It was quite common for the Egyptians to decorate tombs with artwork that depicted people, settings, and animals from everyday life. The dog on the far left looks like a Greyhound; this breed was highly regarded by Egyptians. It was considered a pet, and anyone caught mistreating a Greyhound suffered corporal punishment.

with evil, Greyhounds were highly regarded by Egyptians.

The way Egyptians honored their deceased pets was similar to the way in which they honored deceased family members. Dogs were mummified, often wrapped in colorful linen, and placed in the master's tomb, either on a mat at the foot of the coffin or inside the coffin so they could provide guidance and companionship in the afterlife. Some dogs were mummified and laid to rest in their own elaborate coffins.

Elsewhere in the world, dogs were associated with creation myths. According to an Aztec legend, a god named

This figurine from the Kassite epoch, approximately 1500 B.C. (left), depicts Marduk, the chief god of Babylon, with a watchdog. Mastiff-type dogs were domesticated by Babylonians. Highly prized, these dogs were raised in packs and trained for battle. They also were used for hunting boars and lions and for guarding temples and large estates.

Xolotl, who was represented as a dog or a man with a dog's head, was responsible for creating the various Aztec tribes. While collecting the bones of people who had died, Xolotl incurred the wrath of the Aztec god of death. While trying to outrun the underworld god, Xolotl dropped the bones, causing them to shatter. The pieces scattered, and each became a different tribe.

Other Native Americans, from the Jicarilla Apaches to the Pit River Indians to the Mbaya Indians of South Amer- ica, also believed the dog played a role in creation. In their stories, the dog exists before humans, and often the dog is portrayed as the creator or ancestor of people—a helper and a teacher who brings food, fire, weapons, and speech.

All knowledge, the totality of all questions and all answers, is contained in the dog.
—*Franz Kafka*

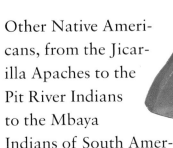

Dogs have played a pivotal role in many societies around the world. Today, dogs are still teaching us the lessons of happiness, forgiveness, and unconditional love.

The figure pictured here is an example of Guatemalan folk art.

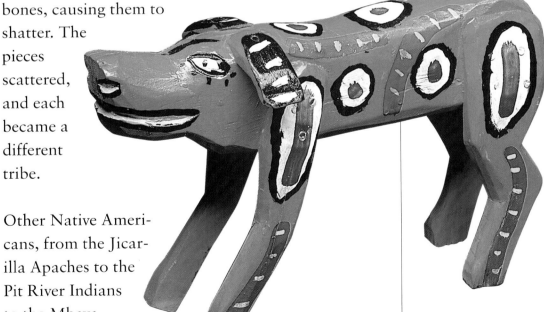

DOGS THROUGH THE AGES

*T*he dog had a special place in many other ancient cultures as well. For instance, in China, the Pekingese was once considered a sacred dog that only the Chinese emperor could own. Anyone caught trying to steal a Pekingese was put to death. The first temple for dogs was built during the Ch'in dynasty (221–207 B.C.). In Japanese mythology, Omisto, the Japanese god of suicide, was thought to have a dog's head. Anyone who killed himself in the name of Omisto was promised eternal joy. As far back as the seventh century A.D., Lhasa Apsos were given a place of honor in Tibetan

The Pekingese has a unique place of honor among dogs. In ancient times, this breed was considered sacred in its homeland of China. The breed can be traced to the eighth-century Tang Dynasty. The Pekingese was the exclusive property of the Chinese Imperial Court—in death as well as in life. Upon a royal master's death, a Pekingese was sacrificed in order to offer protection in the afterlife.

Known in Tibet as Abso Seng Kye, or the "Bark Lion Sentinel Dog," the Lhasa Apso (above) was developed as an indoor guard. While Mastiffs stood watch outside, Lhasas were ever-alert for signs of internal disturbance. Though small in size, the Lhasa was an excellent guard and a wise judge of character. This breed's keen intelligence and strong sense of discernment enabled it to distinguish between those with good and evil intentions.

monasteries. It was believed that monks who had not yet reached Nirvana were reincarnated as Lhasa Apsos. No wonder they treated the little dogs with love and respect! Tibet's spiritual leaders—the Dalai Lamas—often sent Lhasas as gifts to the Chinese imperial court.

Of course, dogs were also valued and mythologized for their more practical aspects. The ancient Greeks especially valued watchdogs. Fierce dogs guarded the temples of Asclepius, and it was believed these dogs could distinguish true Greeks from intruders who dared to enter. In Greek mythology, a monster named Cerberus—a three-headed dog with a dragon's tail and a serpent's head on its back—guarded the gates of the underworld.

The Romans also held great affection for the canine species, and dogs were

Greek mythology is rife with monsters and other creatures, including Cerberus, a three-headed dog with a dragon's tail and a serpent's head on its back. Cerberus is said to have guarded the gates of Hades. This Augusto Pajou sculpture depicts Pluto, the Greek god of the underworld, with his faithful servant Cerberus.

present throughout the age of the Roman Empire. It was with the Romans that the household warning *Cave canem*—Beware of the Dog—originated. A sign of the dog's great value—a value the dog might have preferred to do without—was its use as a sacrificial animal. Dogs were sacrificed at the annual Roman festival of Robigalia: A dog was killed at the fifth milestone on the Via Claudia.

Even some religions held dogs in great esteem. The Persian prophet Zoroaster, founder of Zoroastrianism (circa 1500 B.C.), taught his disciples the importance of dogs, especially shepherds and guard dogs.

Ancient Greeks owned dogs, but until the classical period, dogs were wild, wolflike creatures with erect ears. In time, dogs were domesticated and became important hunting companions who accompanied the Greeks through the rough terrain of Northern Greece. Dogs of Indian origin, who barked when they located game, were especially popular. The dog in this statue (left) gazes attentively at his master.

This mosaic dates back to the ancient city of Pompeii that was destroyed in A.D. 79 by the eruption of Mount Vesuvius. The dog pictured in tile is a symbol of the Roman warning Cave canem, or Beware of the Dog.

The religion taught that a dog's life is as valuable as a human life, and that there are two sins against dogs: giving a dog food that is too hot and denying a dog food while people are eating.

Except for the Spitz types used for hauling and hunting in the northern regions, dogs were unheard of in ancient China. Other breeds were introduced to China as gifts from Westerners to emperors, who apparently took a great liking to the canine species. The emperors kept the gift dogs as pets and, later, used them for hunting. The emperors of the Chow dynasty (1050–249 B.C.) ordered the ambassadors of distant provinces to acquire hunting dogs. The beautiful onyx sculpture pictured below is an early Chinese artisan's tribute to the dog.

According to scripture, punishment for these sins could result in the perpetrator being cast into outer darkness after death.

Not only are stories of dogs included in world religions, but they abound in folklore and mythology as well. There are many tales that describe dog's devotion to man, and many portray the dog as a teacher or an assistant. One fascinating

Chinese story shows how dogs are helpers. In this tale, all the people of the earth were starving as the result of a great flood. Fortunately, someone finally noticed a few seeds caught in a dog's tail. The seeds turned out to be rice, thus giving the people a crop to plant that would feed everyone abundantly. The Chinese tradition of giving the family dog a helping of rice at the beginning of a meal continues today.

In many legends, dogs are praised for their sense of honor and duty, traits for which we still admire them today. A wonderful and somewhat sad tale of devotion is that of a hound who belonged to the

The fidelity of a dog is a precious gift demanding no less binding moral responsiblities than the friendship of a human being. The bond with a true dog is as lasting as the ties of this earth can ever be.

—*Konrad Lorenz*

Dogs held a dual role in Asian society. Some types were petted and pampered by the nobility and lived lives of great ease. These breeds included the Pekingese, Shih Tzu, and Japanese Chin, Toy breeds that were frequently given as tribute to Chinese and Japanese emperors. Others, such as the Chinese Shar-Pei and the Chow Chow, were destined for more harsh fates: the fighting ring or the cooking pot. In this tapestry (right), a young woman offers her dog what appears to be wine from the vessel she is carrying.

12th-century Welsh prince Llewellyn. According to legend, the hound, Gelert, was left at home with the prince's son, Owain. When the prince returned, he found blood on the dog's face and his son was missing. Assuming the worst, the prince killed the dog with his sword. Later, he found his son safe, beside the body of a slain wolf Gelert had killed to protect the boy. In honor of Gelert's bravery, a statue of remembrance was erected.

Numerous other myths, lore, and legends have been passed on over the years—through different cultures, different religions, and different time periods. Dogs have been revered, idolized, respected, worshiped, and sometimes feared. Over time, however, the bond between dogs and mankind has grown ever stronger.

CANINE HEROES

There have been many accounts throughout the ages of dogs behaving in ways that can't be fully explained, specifically when it comes to saving a person's life. Dogs have risked their own lives to save their masters. Why they do so isn't fully understood. But without a doubt, humans can learn from the selfless actions of canine heroes—the selfless actions from which legends grow.

Consider Patches, a Collie/Malamute mix, who saved his owner from certain death by rescuing him from an icy lake and dragging him to safety. Why did Patches risk his own life to save his master? How did Patches know to dive deep into the water, grab his master by the hair, and pull him to safety? Animal behaviorists offer some clues why a dog might risk his

The whole charm of the dog lies in the depth of the friendship and the strength of the spiritual ties with which he has bound himself to man.

—Konrad Lorenz

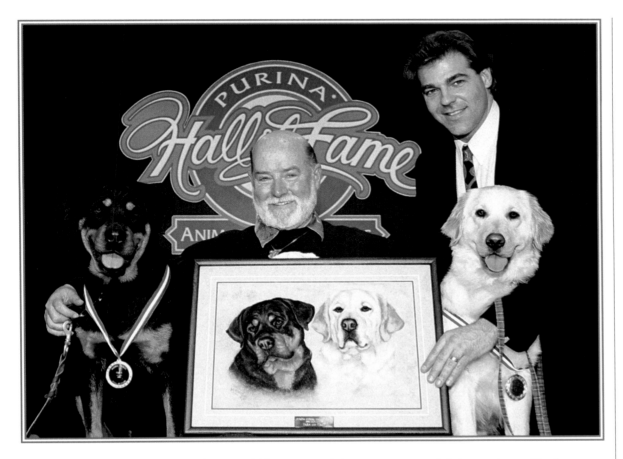

Jim Gilchrist (center) poses with his dogs, Tara (left) and Tiree (right) at the 1996 Purina Animal Hall of Fame awards ceremony. The four-year-old Rottweiler and one-year-old Golden Retriever saved Gilchrist when he fell through the ice on Lake Simcoe in Canada. Tara rushed to help, but she also fell through the ice into the frigid water. Tiree crouched on the ice so Gilchrist could grab her collar. While holding onto Tiree, Gilchrist pulled Tara out. Then the pair worked together to pull their owner to safety.

own life to save his master's life: a close bond, motivation, the ability to read subtle cues. Following that, no one really understands why dogs act heroically. Some say it's because dogs have a sixth sense, which can't really be measured scientifically. Only Patches and the other dogs who risk their lives to save human lives know the real reason. We can only be grateful they love people enough to do so.

Another instance is Eve, the Rottweiler who pulled her disabled owner from a van and into a ditch moments before the vehicle burst into flames. Or T.J., the dog who saved his owners' lives by warning them of a fire in the middle of the night.

Girl saved Ray Ellis's life in 1994. Ellis was cutting trees in the woods near his home when a three-foot sapling sprang up, knocking him out and causing him to drop his chain saw. His left foot was nearly severed. Girl ran home to alert Ellis's wife, who soon followed the German Shepherd Dog into the woods to rescue her husband.

Chester Jenkins poses with Bailey, his Chesapeake Bay Retriever/Labrador mix. The pair have a very special bond, thanks to Bailey's bravery and quick thinking. Bailey tangled with a 2,000-pound Belgian Blue bull when the animal charged Jenkins, knocking him into a watering trough, where the bull pinned him and raked his hooves over the man's back. Bailey diverted the bull's attention, giving Jenkins time to escape.

Patches received the 1965 Ken-L-Ration Dog Hero of the Year award for rescuing his master, Marvin Scott, from drowning in a freezing lake. Dogs of all breeds, shapes, and sizes have been helping humans for generations in everyday life and through heroic measures as well. And in return, humans have thankfully given credit to these canines for saving lives devotedly and tirelessly.

There are many stories of family dogs who jump in the swimming pool to save a toddler, as well as dogs who are able to predict seizures and keep their owner out of harm's way until the episode ends or human help can arrive.

As noted in the New Testament, there is no greater love than that of a man who lays down his life for a friend. Knowing how special dogs are, it's not surprising a dog will show such love by choosing to risk his life to save a friend. True stories such as those of the amazing Patches, Eve, and T.J. prove—yet again—that dogs are truly human-kind's best friend in every way.

Chapter 8

Dogs in the Arts

*Children and dogs are as necessary
to the welfare of the country as
Wall Street and the railroads.*

—*Harry S Truman*

ART

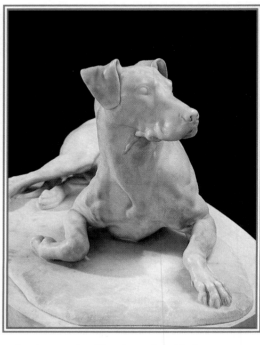

During the 18th century, artists began considering dogs as subjects in their own right rather than as part of the background. This marble sculpture by Pierre Francois Giraud (1783–1836), titled Un Chien, *may have been meant as a memorial to a special dog, for it was also during this time that wealthy people began to bury their pets with the same type of monuments they used for their own tombs.*

*C*anis familiaris has infiltrated every aspect of human life, including the books we read, movies and television shows we watch, and art exhibits we enjoy. Given the dog's good looks, natural talent, and awesome personality, it's easy to understand why canines have inspired countless writers, producers, and artists. It's been said that art imitates life, and—in the case of dogs in the arts—this phrase certainly rings true. Dogs are so much a part of everyday human life, it would be unusual, even odd, if they weren't showcased in creative projects of all sorts.

Dog lovers especially appreciate artistic

Previous page:
A Dog, *by Francisco José de Goya y Lucientes.*

The poor dog, in life the firmest friend,
The first to welcome, foremost to defend.
—Lord Byron

During the Middle Ages, the hunt evolved into a lavish, complex ritual that included the use of many dogs. Because of the societal importance of the hunt, it was a common tapestry subject in the late Middle Ages and during the Renaissance. This 15th-century tapestry depicts the hunt for a unicorn, which reputedly could be captured only by a virgin. Each animal in the tapestry has a symbolic meaning. Dogs generally symbolize fidelity; from the Latin word fidelis, meaning faithful, comes the dog name Fido.

Portraits of dogs often symbolize the times in which they were painted as well as the social status of the owners. They can reflect differing economic levels, class struggles, and cultural fads. Pictured is an oil on canvas of Royal, a tricolor Springer Spaniel, by British artist Lilian Cheviot (1894–1930).

painted, repainted, and painted again, dog lovers never tire of seeing their canine friends immortalized in a sketch. With the exception of the horse, the dog has been portrayed on canvas more than any other animal in history.

Artistic tributes to the dog may be pure pleasure, but they can also serve a more practical

tributes to the canine species. Dogs comprise a subject that is never boring, never old. There can never be too many stories about dogs or too many paintings depicting dogs. While some people might tire of seeing a bowl of fruit

In addition to the intelligence dogs demonstrated in their ability to learn tricks and commands, it was canine maternal devotion that suggested to 18th-century thinkers that perhaps dogs were capable of emotions similar to those of humans. Mother's Pride, by 19th-century artist Raymonde Lynde, suggests just such devotion.

purpose. Many times, tracing the history of a particular breed is difficult. Looking to the arts, which often reflect a particular time period, can help breed historians piece together a map of the past. For example, drawings by the German artist Albrecht Dürer date the Poodle to the 15th and 16th centuries; while paintings by the Spanish artist Goya show the Poodle as a popular pet in late-18th-century Spain. One particular oil painting from England (circa 1864) depicts an Irish Water Spaniel named Rake, who is viewed by breed historians as a contemporary Irish Water Spaniel. Rake was a descendent of Boatswain, the famous

In addition to using dogs to capture the essence of a social milieu, artists used dogs to symbolize changes in society, or even to suggest a community's spirit, as does Man With a Parasol *(right) by Impressionist artist Claude Monet (1840–1926).*

As an author and illustrator of several zoology and anatomy works, George Stubbs (1724–1806) brought exacting qualities to his myriad canine portraits. Considered one of the finest animal painters of his century, Stubbs used all breeds of dogs, horses, and other domestic animals, as well as a cheetah and a kangaroo, as his subjects. This portrait of A Hound and Bitch in a Landscape shows Stubbs's ability to capture the dog's physical likeness while expressing its special nature.

sire of many outstanding show and gundogs.

The artist George Stubbs, who rightly holds the title of the 18th century's greatest animal painter, is famous for his paintings of sporting dogs and horses, but he did not limit himself to these subjects. One of his well-known paintings is titled *White Poodle in a Punt*, and it displays all the detail and personality that Stubbs brought to his art. Another 18th-century great, portrait artist Thomas Gainsborough, is also known for his paintings of animals. A Bull Terrier named Bumper is the subject of Gainsborough's earliest surviving work, and he is well

It was not unusual for now-famous artists such as Monet to accept commissions for dog portraits. Like struggling artists in any era, they did what was necessary to survive. Sometimes dogs and their people were painted together, often displaying the uncanny way in which dogs and their owners tend to resemble one another. Claude Monet, Mme. Paul Patissiere (detail).

inspired by the fidelity and courage of dogs, and thanks to his position as court painter for Queen Victoria and Prince Albert—great pet lovers themselves—his work helped spread the new notion that animals had feelings like our own and were deserving of a higher place in people's hearts.

American pop culture artist Andy Warhol was influenced by his two miniature Dachshunds, Amos and Archie, who shared his bed and made cameo appearances in his art. This portrait of Amos, a candid head shot, is an oil on canvas painted in 1976.

Two Tahitian Girls and a Dog, by Paul Gauguin (1848–1903), is one of this renowned artist's many interesting works. It is perhaps not surprising that this dog's expression is quizzical as he watches the woman approach; as in Asian societies, dogs in the Pacific Islands were often used as food. Still Life With Three Puppies (1888) is another Gauguin painting with a canine subject.

known for his painting of a Pomeranian and her puppy, on display at London's Tate Gallery. But it was during the Victorian era that dogs came into their own as the subjects of paintings. Artist Sir Edwin Landseer is perhaps the best known of the Victorian animal portraitists. His art was often

Although its creator, Francis Barraud (1856–1924), lies in obscurity, His Master's Voice *is one of the best known of all dog pictures, not to mention one of the most frequently reproduced. The painting is said to have been inspired by the artist's pet terrier Nipper, who was terribly puzzled upon hearing the sound of a familiar voice on a phonograph. The Royal Academy rejected* His Master's Voice *when it was submitted for exhibition, but Barraud sold the image to The Gramophone Company after changing the phonograph in the original to the newer-model gramophone that the company produced. American rights to the famous dog and phonograph were acquired by RCA in 1929.*

FILM AND TELEVISION

*A*side from looking to the arts to understand specific breeds, we look to them to simply enjoy a tribute to the canine species. The paintings of the past that captured so many dogs have given way to a 20th-century medium: film. And dogs have been right there making their presence known in movies and television shows.

One of the first, and almost forgotten, canine movie stars is Strongheart, a beautiful German Shepherd from champion stock. Strongheart achieved stardom in a 1921 epic titled *The Silent Call*. Strongheart played a dog that was half wolf—and extremely intelligent. But, as fate would have it, the famous Strongheart was soon playing second fiddle to another German Shepherd, this one named Rin Tin Tin. "Rinty," as he was affectionately called, first appeared in a 1923 film, *Where the North Begins*.

This early photograph of "Rinty," as he was often called (opposite page), *shows the television star of* The Adventures of Rin Tin Tin. *The handsome German Shepherd Dog captured the hearts of children and adults alike, and he was nothing less than a hero for many. For baby boomers who grew up watching the television series, sweet childhood memories and Rin Tin Tin go hand in hand.*

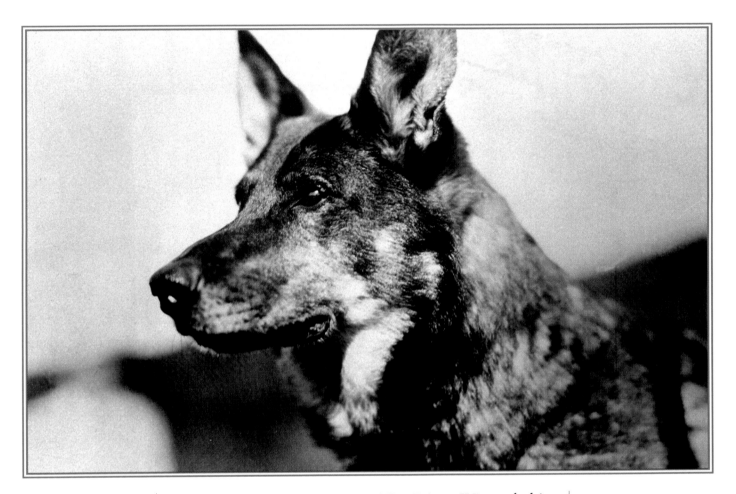

The public's love affair with Rin Tin Tin lasted many years, and several generations of dogs enjoyed a celebrity's life while playing this part. In 1954, when the television era arrived, Rin Tin Tin (Rinty IV) made his presence felt on the small screen as well, in a series titled *The Adventures of Rin Tin Tin*.

One of the first "boy and his dog"-type

the boy that life doesn't always offer what seems acceptable. A few years later, Disney produced another boy-and-his-dog story, *Big Red* (1962), about a beautiful, show-quality Irish Setter.

Lassie's fame began with the book by Eric Knight. A film version, Lassie Come Home, *followed, and it was the beginning of decades of popularity for the beloved Collie. The first Lassie television series had one of the longest runs ever—17 years.*

Arliss Coates (played by Kevin Corcoran) hugs Old Yeller, the stray dog who came to live with his family in Texas in 1869. Old Yeller was released Christmas Day, 1957, and was extremely successful. It received glowing reviews from critics and grossed eight million dollars. The film has continued to be loved by generations of dog lovers since.

motion pictures was Disney's tremendously popular *Old Yeller* (1957). Old Yeller, played by the real life Spike, is the touching story of a big yellow dog who comes to live with a Texas family whose 15-year-old son becomes extremely attached to him. Sadly, Yeller contracts rabies and has to be humanely destroyed. Yeller's death teaches

Walt Disney's Lady and the Tramp *has delighted generations of children since its release in 1955, but it certainly didn't entertain the critics of the day. The cartoon's success proved that the public disagreed—not surprising, since with its mutt vs. purebred metaphor,* Lady and the Tramp *embodies the conflicts in great romances such as* Romeo and Juliet *and* West Side Story, *albeit with Disney's trademark happy ending.*

The magnificent Collie, Lassie, became a star when *Lassie Comes Home* was released in 1943. Backed by a star-studded cast including Elizabeth Taylor, Roddy McDowall, and Edmund Gwenn, the movie and the canine star were a success. And they stayed that way through myriad Lassie sequels, a television series, and several generations of

Collies who played the part of Lassie.

The story of Benji is certainly that of rags to riches. The mixed breed traces his humble beginnings to a shelter in Burbank, California. Benji (formerly Higgins) got his start on the television series *Petticoat Junction*, then starred in several hit films, including *Benji* and *For the Love of Benji*.

Pongo, Perdita, and a few of the 101 Dalmatian puppies from the 1961 Disney cartoon (above). The feature-length cartoon was made possible due to new technology called Xerography. This allowed animators to make multiple copies of drawings, eliminating the need to draw 101 separate dogs. In 1996, Disney released a live-action version of the film, introducing a new generation to an updated version of the classic story.

Other popular canine stars are *The Wizard of Oz*'s Toto, a Cairn Terrier; the huge and handsome Beethoven, a cuddly Saint Bernard from the motion picture of the same name; Spuds MacKenzie, a Bull Terrier made famous in beer commercials; Eddie, the intelligent and comic Jack Russell Terrier on the television sitcom *Frazier*; and, of course, all 101 of Disney's lovable Dalmatians.

Each of these movies and television shows brings a breed to life for the generation that discovers it. In the 1950s and 1960s, Collies and Irish Setters zoomed to the top of the charts in popularity. The same, in

Most people have a favorite character from The Wizard of Oz, but Dorothy (Judy Garland) and Toto (left) are probably the two best loved by audiences. Toto, a cute, scrappy Cairn Terrier, was perfect for his part in the movie. It's difficult to imagine another breed sharp enough to outsmart a wicked witch!

Not only have dogs starred in their own films and television shows, they have also been the pampered pets of movie and TV stars. Pictured are Jack Benny and a Great Dane; Oprah Winfrey and her Cocker Spaniel Soloman; Bob Hope with a Great Dane and a Chihuahua; John F. Kennedy, Jr., Caroline Bessette Kennedy, and their dog, Friday; Madonna and her Chihuahua; Humphrey Bogart, Captain Kid, and two Scotties; Elizabeth Taylor and Sugar; and Grace Kelly and a Great Dane. These animals are hardly star struck, though. The trappings of the beautiful life don't mean much to the canine mind. Dogs are just as devoted to plain-Jane owners as they are to rich and famous celebrities.

appeal of television and movies because they are comforting and familiar icons, and their presence adds an extra measure of reality to the story being told, making it easy for viewers to identify with the characters and situations on screen.

Long before Rin Tin Tin and Lassie, movie producers recognized the value of including dogs in films. One look at the dashing Jiggs, a canine star from the 1920s, outfitted in goggles, pipe, and thick collar, will elicit a chuckle from anyone. Jiggs's passenger seems unconcerned about this canine's driving record!

Even a President's pets attract media attention! Fala, the favored Scottish Terrier of President Franklin Delano Roosevelt, poses for a trio of reporters sent to the White House to photograph the terrier on his birthday (April 7, 1942). It wasn't long before Fala, true to his tough Scottish heritage, took charge of the session and snapped a few stills of his own.

turn, happened with Dalmatians and Jack Russell Terriers in the 1990s. The silver screen and television can make a dog seem larger than life, the perfect pet for every American family. Of course, we all know this isn't necessarily the case, but nevertheless, those dogs sure are appealing. Why? Dogs contribute to the broad

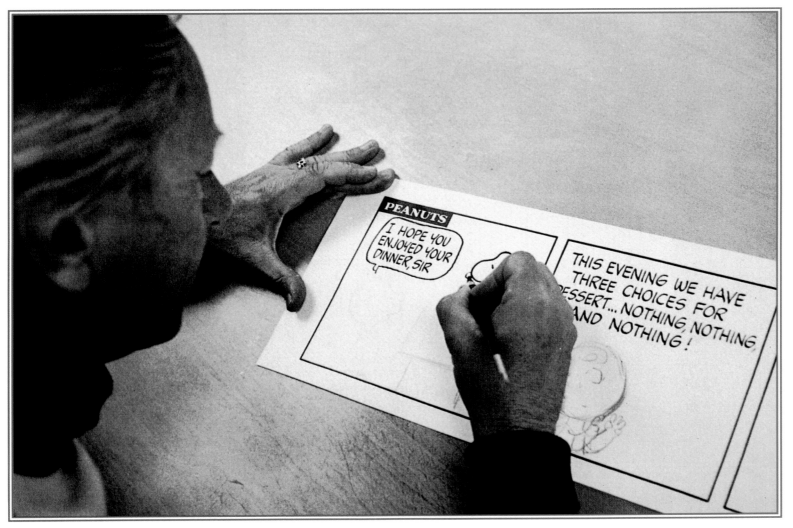

Charles M. Schulz works on an image of Snoopy in his California studio. Snoopy, the Beagle comic-strip character, has appeared daily in newspapers since 1950, entertaining and delighting fans of all ages. This pen-and-ink Beagle shares his life with fellow comic-strip character Charlie Brown and the rest of the Peanuts gang. Snoopy has taken on a life of his own, with a line of stuffed animals and greeting cards and appearances in television specials and life-insurance commercials.

LITERATURE

Greyhound coursing has been a popular sport over the centuries. This detail (above) *from the* Canterbury Tales *by Geoffrey Chaucer (1342–1400) pictures a worldly monk and his Greyhounds. In Chaucer's tale, the monk spent all his time and money hunting hares instead of attending to his priestly duties.*

The public loves watching dogs on screen, but long before film came along, dogs starred in the pages of books. As a matter of fact, more than a few popular movies started out as books. Knowing this, throughout the ages writers have spun tales, poems, and novels that have included dogs, are about dogs, or just have a dog passing through.

Scottish novelist and poet Sir Walter Scott penned a touching tribute to the dog in *The Talisman* (1832). Scott reminds the reader that dogs are a gift from above; "Recollect that

The psychological and moral comfort of a presence at once humble and understanding— this is the greatest benefit that the dog has bestowed upon man.

—Percy Bysshe Shelley

the Almighty... gave the dog to be companion of our pleasures and our toils," and describes the wonderful, noble nature of the dog. Dog lovers will agree with his observation that dogs are "incapable of deceit."

Another tribute to the dog can be found in an essay entitled *Bedfellows,* by the witty E.B. White. White fondly remembers his Dachshund, Fred, who for many years "always attended the sick, climbing right into bed with the patient." White describes the dog's somewhat peculiar sense of humor, poking fun at his own attachment to a companion who was "red and low-posted and longbodied."

This portrait of Alexander Pope and his dog, Bounce, was painted by Jonathan Richardson in 1718. Pope is famous among dog lovers for the epigram—engraved on the collar of a dog of one of the children of George I—"I am his Highness' dog at Kew; Pray tell me, sir, whose dog are you?"

E.B. White, author of One Man's Meat *(1942),* Here is New York *(1949), and* Charlotte's Web *(1952), was a dog lover as well as an accomplished writer. He was especially fond of Dachshunds as a breed, and more particularly, of his own Dachshund, Fred, whom he immortalized in the essay* Bedfellows.

In fact, Fred's grave is the only grave that White visited with any regularity—a habit he himself described as odd but understandable.

The gifted writer O. Henry wrote a clever piece from a dog's point of view, *Memoirs of a Yellow Dog*, in which the narrator described himself as being born a "yellow pup; date, locality, pedigree and weight unknown." In this funny story, a dog imparts wisdom to his master.

Hunters throughout the ages have had dogs as companions, and writer-journalist Ernest Hemingway was no slouch as a hunter. Here, Hemingway (left), film star Gary Cooper (center), a friend, and two Labrador Retrievers rest a moment during a hunting trip. Hemingway wrote such works as The Sun Also Rises *(1926),* A Farewell to Arms *(1929), and* For Whom the Bell Tolls *(1940).*

In John Steinbeck's timeless novel, *Travels With Charley*, readers enjoy the adventures of the author and Charley, his Standard Poodle, as they travel across the United States. Charley is known for being quiet natured and tolerant.

Steinbeck's novel captures the unique bonding and friendship that often takes place between dog and human.

In 1807, poet William Wordsworth wrote *Fidelity* (from *Poems in Two Volumes*), a wonderful poem that tells the sad story of a man named Charles Gough who set out one early spring day, accompanied by his dog, to go fishing. Gough slipped while hiking to his destination and died. His faithful dog, however, stayed by his side some three months, whining and whimpering. How did the dog survive all that time? As Wordsworth writes, it was due to the dog's "strength of feeling, great Above all human estimate!" Interestingly, Sir Walter Scott heard of the accident and also penned a tribute (*Hellvellyn*, 1805) to the faithful dog.

Pulitzer- and Nobel Prize-winning writer John Steinbeck shared his life with many dogs, but perhaps the best known is Charley, his much-loved Standard Poodle. In his 1961 book Travels With Charley, *Steinbeck chronicles their journey through the United States; an attempt, he said, "to rediscover my people." This photo* (left), *taken in 1962, shows Steinbeck and Charley strolling the grounds of their California home.*

Eugene O'Neill (1888–1953) relaxes with a Dalmatian friend in 1937 (right). This 20th-century American playwright was a four-time winner of the Pulitzer Prize and 1936 winner of the Nobel Prize for literature. For dog lovers, however, O'Neill is perhaps better known for The Last Will and Testament of Silverdene Emblem O'Neill, *the musings of a dog facing death. It contains the comforting lines: "No matter how deep my sleep I shall hear you, and not all the power of death can keep my spirit from wagging its grateful tail."*

To Flush, My Dog, written by renowned poet Elizabeth Barrett Browning (1843), speaks not only of an owner's love of a pet, but of a dog who was much more than a friend. Browning was an invalid, and Flush was her faithful bedside companion for 14 years. She fondly describes the Cocker Spaniel's coat "Like a lady's ringlets brown, Flow thy silken ears adown" and proclaims "But of thee it shall be said, This dog watched beside a bed Day and night unweary." Barrett Browning's adoration for her loving canine companion is surely shared by thousands of people whose dogs comfort them as they lie confined to a bed at home or in a nursing facility.

A favorite author of all animal lovers is English veterinarian James Her-

The more I see of men, the better I like dogs.
—Mme Roland

Wishbone, the Jack Russell Terrier of public television, brings classic literature to life for kids every day, helping them to relive the adventures of heroes such as Romeo (opposite page), Robin Hood, and Odysseus. The use of a dog in these roles can help foster an interest in the stories for young viewers who aren't familiar with Shakespeare, Sherwood Forest, or ancient Greece.

riot. *All Creatures Great and Small* is probably his best-known novel, but he wrote several others, including *James Herriot's Dog Stories* (1986). Within that volume is the account of Rip (*The Lame Dog*), the working dog of a farmer named Jack. Rip suffers an injury to his right foreleg, which doesn't heal. Then the unfortunate dog is hit by a car, fracturing his hind leg on the same side. As time goes on, the prognosis worsens because the

hind leg won't heal. However, Jack refuses to accept that his beloved Rip won't be able to work. He packs up his family and drives off to church to say a prayer for Rip. Miraculously, Rip learns to move using only his left legs. This is an inspirational tale of the power of love and faith.

The dogs we see in television shows and in movies and read about in books can be as real to us—and as dear—as real-life canine companions. The fact that writers and artists are able to capture the essence of the canine species is especially dear to dog lovers, who never tire of seeing a tribute to a four-legged friend.

Recollect that the Almighty, who gave the dog to be companion of our pleasures and our toils, hath invested him with a nature noble and incapable of deceit.

—*Sir Walter Scott*

Photo Credits:

Front cover: **Brian Warling Photography.**

Back cover: **SuperStock:** (left); **Tetsu Yamazaki:** (top & right).

Animals Animals: Henry Ausloos: 65 (top), 120 (bottom), 143 (bottom); Michael Habicht: 149; Gérard Lacz: 42 (top), 58 (bottom); Robert Pearcy: 44 (top), 144; Fritz Prenzel: 74; Michael & Barbara Reed: 4 (bottom), 59 (top); Ralph A. Reinhold: 45, 119 (top); **Archive Photos:** 202, 203, 204, 205 (top left, top right center, bottom left center, & bottom right), 207; Big Pictures: 205 (bottom left); Herbert: 201; Lee: 205 (top left center); **Art Resource:** Bridgeman Art Library, London: 176, 184, 209; Giraudon: 175, 195; Erich Lessing: 173; Scala: 174, 182, 183, 185, 191; Tate Gallery, London: 196; Andy Warhol Foundation, Inc.: 198 (bottom); **Bettmann Archive:** 199; Corbis: 27, 178, 181 (bottom), 197, 206, 210, 211, 212, 213; **Big Feast! Entertainment:** 214, 215; **Laura Cavanaugh/Globe Photos, Inc.:** 205 (top right); **Culver Pictures, Inc.:** 25; **Kent & Donna Dannen:** 3, 17, 18, 20, 21, 28, 40, 42 (bottom), 43 (center), 53, 54 (top), 55 (bottom), 59 (bottom right), 70 (bottom), 72, 85, 86, 87, 89, 91, 96, 99, 102 (top), 105, 106, 108, 109 (top), 111, 113, 115, 118, 132, 136, 138, 142, 145, 146, 153, 157, 158, 159, 160, 162 (top), 166 (bottom), 180, 181 (top); **Delta Society, Renton, WA:** 169, 170; **Manuel Denner/International Stock:** 33; **FPG International:** 156; Adamsmith Productions: 71 (top), 167; Alan Bergman: 165 (top); Ron Chapple: 164 (bottom); Jim Cummins: 168; Jerry Driendl: 104; Richard Gaul: 101, 112 (bottom); Steven Gottlieb: 109 (bottom); Larry Grant: 16 (top), 161, 162 (bottom); Don Herbert: 127; Michael Kornafel: 78; Barbara Leslie: 128; Bill Losh: 84, 165 (bottom); Mike Malyszko: 31, 114; Diane Padys: 80; Richard Price: 131; G. Randall: 83, 90; Stephanie Rausser: 123, 129, 134; Ken Reid: 32; Mark Reinstein: 166 (top); Ron Rovtar: 155; H. Schlapfer: 43 (bottom); A. Schmidecker: 37 (bottom), 71 (bottom); Michael Simpson: 5 (center), 150; Stephen Simpson: 100, 125; Walter Smith: 135 (top); Andrea Sperling: 98; Jeffrey Sylvester: 102 (bottom); Ed Taylor Studio: 126; Larry West: 75; **Rose Hartman/Photoplay Archives/LGI Photo Agency:** 205 (bottom right center); **Courtesy of Heinz Pet Products:** 188, 189; **Photri, Inc.:** 15, 16 (bottom), 19, 29, 41, 121, 135 (bottom); Larry Allan: 39; D&I MacDonald: 140; Microstock: 46; MGA: 38, 147; Michael Philip Manheim: 67; **Purina Animal Hall of Fame:** 187; **Rainbow:** Tom McCarthy: 82; Frank Siteman: 88, 171; **Seeing Eye:** 154; **Sterling Photography:** 137; **SuperStock:** title page, 9 (top), 11 (bottom); 34, 35, 37 (top), 44 (bottom), 47, 49, 51, 52, 54 (bottom), 56, 57, 62, 64, 66, 70 (top), 73, 77, 79, 81, 97, 103, 107, 112 (top), 116, 117, 119 (bottom), 120 (top), 130, 133, 139, 141, 143 (top), 148, 151, 163; Art Trade, Bonhams, London/Bridgeman Art Library, London: 194 (bottom); Leonid Bogdanov/Hermitage Museum, St. Petersburg, Russia: 22; British Museum, London/ Bridgeman Art Library, London: 177; Christie's Images: 26, 194 (top); Civic Museum, Oderzo, Italy/ET Archive, London: 23; D. Fox: 8 (top); Silvio Fiore/Museum of Baghdad, Baghdad, Iraq: 24 (bottom); Hermitage Museum, St. Petersburg, Russia/Giraudon: 198 (top); Tom Holton: 179; Huntington Library, Art Collections, and Botanical Gardens, San Marino, California: 208; Musee de Cluny, Paris: 193; Musee du Louvre, Giraudon: 192; Donald Nuccis/Valley of the Kings, Dier El Bahri, Egypt: 13; Kurt Scholz: 24 (top); Jerry Shulman: 63; **Tetsu Yamazaki:** 4 (top), 5 (top & bottom), 6, 7, 8 (bottom), 9 (bottom), 10, 11 (top), 36, 48, 50, 55 (top), 58 (top), 59 (bottom top right), 60, 61, 64 (top), 65 (bottom), 68, 69, 92, 93, 95, 164 (top), photo credits page.